# NORTHWEST PASSAGE

# NORTHWEST PASSAGE

## THE QUEST FOR AN ARCTIC ROUTE TO THE EAST

TEXT BY EDWARD STRUZIK
PHOTOGRAPHY BY MIKE BEEDELL

KEY PORTER BOOKS

A detail from H.M.S. *Assistance* and *Pioneer* Breaking Out of Winter Quarters, *sketched by Walter W. May. The break-up occurred suddenly in dense fog, and many articles that had been stored on the ice were carried away.*

**Canadian Cataloguing in Publication Data**

Struzik, Edward, 1954-
  Northwest Passage

ISBN 1-55013-181-8

1. Northwest Passage—Discovery and exploration.
I. Beedell, Mike, 1956- . II. Title.

G640.S85 1990   910'.916327   C90-093709-2

Key Porter Books Limited
70 The Esplanade
Toronto, Ontario
M5E 1R2

Distributed in the United States of America
by Publishers Group West
4065 Hollis Street, Emeryville
California 94608, 1-800-365-3453.

The Publisher wishes to thank the following people for their contributions: Laurie Coulter, Ian Darragh, Dr. A.T. Davidson and George Hobson

*Design:* Scott Richardson
*Cartography:* Steven Fick/Canadian Geographic
*Typesetting:* Techni Process Lettering Limited

Printed on acid-free paper
Printed and bound in Italy

91 92 93 94 95 96 6 5 4 3 2 1

*Page i:*

*Paddling on a calm sea near Pelly Bay, an Inuit hamlet on the eastern Arctic coast.*

*Page ii:*

*A storm brews on Bylot Island, which guards the entrance to Lancaster Sound. The island was named for Robert Bylot, who sailed with Henry Hudson and William Baffin.*

# CONTENTS

*Summer breakup at an Inuit camp called Sidlerosik on the northeast coast of Baffin Island.*

"If you wish to know what men seek in this land, or why men journey thither in so great danger to their lives, then it is the threefold nature of man which draws him thither. One part of him is emulation and desire of fame.... Another part is the desire of knowledge.... The third part is the desire of gain...."
—FROM *THE KING'S MIRROR*, BY AN UNKNOWN
NORSEMAN, CIRCA 1250

# INTRODUCTION

In 1983, the owners of the cruise ship *Lindblad Explorer* offered a luxury voyage through the Northwest Passage in Canada's Arctic Archipelago. Because of the risk of the ship's being turned back by treacherous ice floes, the New York-based company, which had organized similar adventure tours to the Amazon and the Antarctic, advertised the voyage as one that "would or would not make it." Despite that risk, ninety-eight "sophisticated international travellers" each handed over between $16,900 and $23,000, and the following summer, with ninety-eight bottles of Dom Pérignon champagne aboard, the vessel completed the 4790-mile (7712-km) journey from St. John's, Newfoundland, to Point Barrow, Alaska, in just twenty-three days.

The apparent ease with which the *Lindblad Explorer* navigated the Northwest Passage stands in dramatic contrast to the hardships that beset the search for the route over its 500-year history. From the time John Cabot first set off from Bristol in 1497 in the small bark *Matthew* with a northwest passage to the Orient in mind to the moment almost 350 years later when all 129 crew members of John Franklin's 1845 expedition disappeared, more than 140 vessels and a handful of overland expeditions had tried and failed in the same endeavor. Another thirty-two ships participated in the Franklin search between 1848 and 1859, making it the longest and most expensive search-and-rescue effort in history. Not until Roald Amundsen's *Gjoa* steamed into Lancaster Sound and Barrow Strait in 1903, and rounded Point Barrow, three years later, was the Northwest Passage successfully navigated.

*The northern lights, or aurora borealis, ignite a September sky.*

Few of the men on those earlier voyages savored anything as luxurious as champagne. Franklin, who had arranged for silverware, a 1700-book library, a mahogany desk, copies of *Punch*, and epicurean delights for his fateful voyage, was an exception. The diet for the most part was routine fare—musky-smelling beer, salted pork and beef (tinned meats later on), rotting potatoes, and dried cabbage. Such were the rations, not for twenty-three days, but for a period of from three months to as many as five years, as long as it took to complete the passage or to break free of the ice that frequently held ships captive.

One consequence of the miserable food on prolonged voyages was the onset of scurvy, a life-threatening affliction marked by bleeding gums, loosening teeth, and fatigue, followed by stiffening joints, acute diarrhea, and internal bleeding. Another of the consequences could have been lead poisoning, apparently caused by the solder used on meat tins during the Franklin era. Not only did it compound the physical effects of scurvy, it also very likely caused disorders like paranoia and anorexia, thus affecting the explorers' ability to make rational decisions.

And then there were the discomforts brought on by the Arctic winter. The only clothing supplied was made from regulation wool and broadcloth designed for more moderate climates. Typically, in the Arctic, the sun "sets" in mid-November and remains hidden below the horizon for about three months, leaving captain and crew with only twilight and candlelight to illuminate their activities. Temperatures that routinely plunged to $-40°F$ ($-40°C$), even $-76°F$ ($-60°C$) on occasion, often confined the explorers to their ships, where they tried to heat their cramped quarters with a coal stove and red-hot cannon balls. The effect was not always as comfortable as one might expect. A temperature of $59°F$ ($15°C$) inside a drafty ship's cabin inevitably led to serious condensation problems. Sheets of ice would build up on cold ceilings, and moisture permeated blankets and clothing. Washing meant drying off with a frozen towel that scraped the skin; sleep was often a frustrating exercise of tossing and turning to keep warm and waking up every two hours to calm the shivering.

As repelling a place as the Arctic could be, it was also inspiring and beautiful. Mirages, the aurora borealis, parhelia (mock suns), and white-outs both confused and fascinated the explorers, while polynyas, polygons, pingos, prehistoric-looking muskoxen, and herds of caribou 50 000-strong left them tongue-tied when trying to describe to people back home what they had observed. The sublimity of it all, of course, partly explains why the narratives of the Northwest Passage explorers often out-sold more traditional literary fare, and inspired a number of important literary works and paintings, including Samuel Taylor Coleridge's "The Rime of the Ancient Mariner," Mary Shelley's *Frankenstein*, and Caspar David Friedrich's famous painting *Die gescheiterte Hoffnung* (*The Wreck of Hope*).

Perhaps the inherent mystery associated with the Arctic also explains why international interest in the Northwest Passage continues to this day. Since Amundsen's landmark journey in 1903 – 06, there have been at least thirty-six full transits of the Northwest Passage, including those by a Royal Canadian Mounted Police (RCMP) schooner (in both directions), a Netherlands ketch, a Japanese sloop, a Bahamas-registered passenger ship, a French sailing ship, a U.S. motor yacht, a hydrographic-research vessel, several U.S. Navy sub-

*Jeff MacInnis and Mike Beedell sail their catamaran,* Perception, *near Cape Bathurst in the western Arctic. During the summers of 1986 and 1988, the pair successfully navigated the Passage from Tuktoyaktuk to Pond Inlet, using the wind and muscle power alone. Often, when there was no open water, they had to push their craft over the ice.*

marines, and a variety of ice-breakers and commercial tankers. There have been seventeen partial transits as well.

Despite its enduring notoriety, the Northwest Passage is not as easily defined as one might expect. In geographical terms, it may be described as simply as in the government publication, *Sailing Directions, Arctic Canada,* which refers to a route "that spans the North American Arctic from Davis Strait in Baffin Bay in the east to Bering Strait in the west." In fact, this definition might include any number of passageways through the maze of islands that forms the archipelago if it were not for the fact that 80 percent of the Arctic Ocean in northern Canada is covered with a permanent cap of ice. Taking this into account, only five routes to date have been deemed practicable for navigation. Of these, only two are suitable for deep-draft ships.

Because the notion of a northwest passage was initially based on primitive and sometimes flawed views of the geography of the world, the choice of routes more often evolved out of a process of elimination and the dictates of nature than out of any rational understanding of where the routes to the Orient might lie. In the sixteenth and seventeenth centuries, the focus of the search for the Northwest Passage was Hudson Bay. Many explorers of the time, however, were just as optimistic about finding a northeast passage around Eurasia along the Siberian coast or a more northerly route over the north geographic pole. After repeated failures in all three directions, the search for a northwest passage in the eighteenth and nineteenth centuries developed a three-pronged approach—westward into Barrow Strait by way of Lancaster Sound, eastward

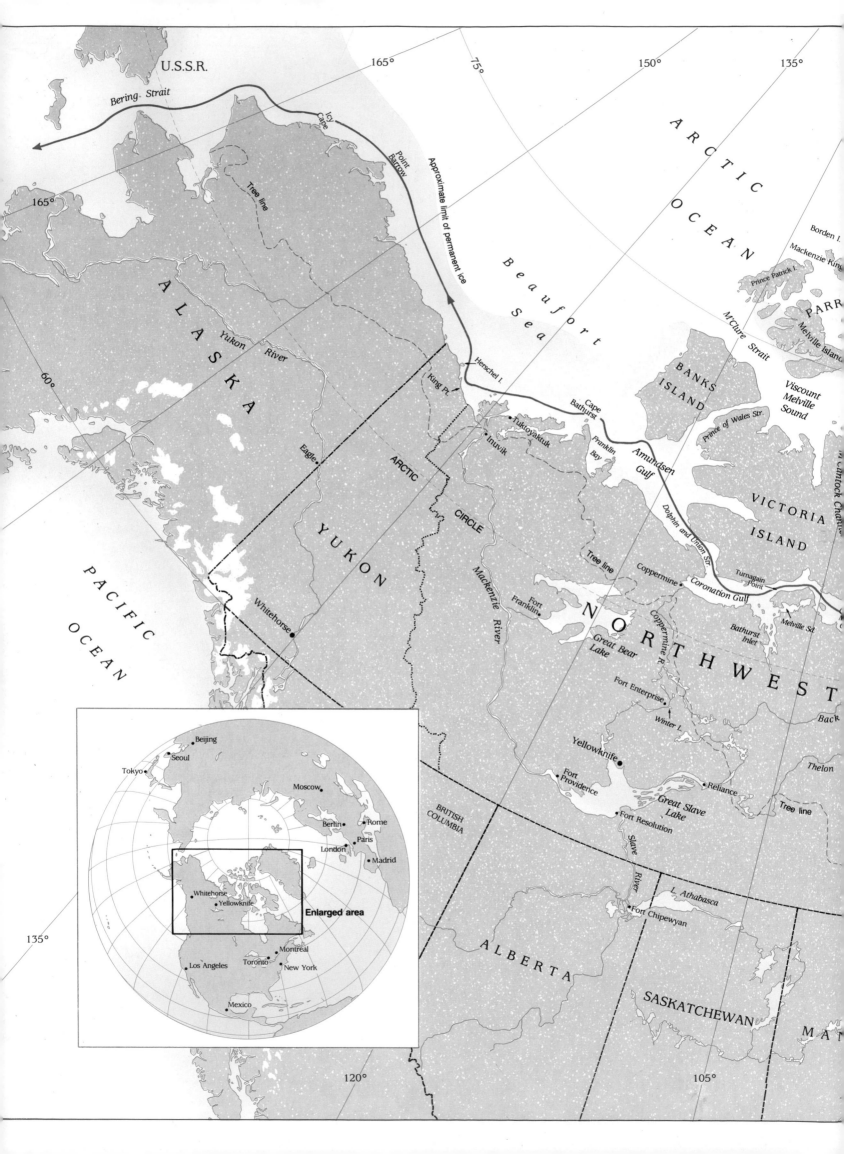

## ROALD AMUNDSEN'S ROUTE (1903–06)

0   100   200   300 km
0       100       200 mi

0°      105°      90°      75°      60°      45°      30°      15°

**SVERDRUP IS.**

Ellef Ringnes I.

**NORTH
△ MAGNETIC
POLE**

Amund Ringnes I.

**ISLANDS**

Axel
Heiberg
Island

**E L L E S M E R E   I S L A N D**

Kane Basin

Smith Sound

Etah

75°

**G R E E N L A N D**

Penny Strait

Bathurst
I.

Grinnell
Pen.

Dundas
I.

Jones Sound

Grise Fiord

North
Water

30°

Cornwallis I.

Devon Island

Resolute

Barrow Str.

Lancaster Sound

ARCTIC  CIRCLE

Prince
of
Wales
Island

Peel Sound

Beechey
I.

Somerset
Island

Prince
Leopold
I.

Prince Regent Inlet

Navy
Board
Inlet

Bylot
I.

Pond Inlet

Disko
I.

Godhavn

45°

Fury Pt.

Brodeur
Pen.

B a f f i n

Franklin Str.

Bellot Str.

Larsen
Out.

Boothia
Peninsula

Gulf
of
Boothia

B a y

D a v i s   S t r a i t

C. Félix

✕ Site of Franklin's death

King
William
I.

Lord Mayor Bay

**B A F F I N   I S L A N D**

Gjoa Haven

Ogle
Pt.

Pelly Bay

Committee
Bay

Prince
Charles
I.

Chantrey
Inlet

Melville
Peninsula

Cumberland Sound.

60°

Roald
Amundsen's
route 1903–1906

River

**T E R R I T O R I E S**

Foxe
Basin

Repulse
Bay

Probisher Bay

River

Wager
Bay

Roes Welcome Sd.

Southampton
Island

Chesterfield Inlet

H u d s o n   S t r a i t

**A T L A N T I C
O C E A N**

Coats
I.

Mansel
I.

Ungava
Bay

L a b r a d o r

**H U D S O N

B A Y**

Churchill

Tree line

**Q U E B E C**

N

**O B A**

Churchill River

Nelson R.

Hayes River

90°  **ONTARIO**

75°

**NEWFOUNDLAND**

60°

from the Pacific Ocean through Bering Strait, and, for a short time, overland across the wilds of North America.

Over the years, the reasons for exploring the Northwest Passage changed as well. Initially, the goal was to make a profit—to find a commercial route to the markets of the Orient. That plan never completely died, but once it proved too risky and expensive for private speculators, finding a northwest passage served as a vehicle for national prestige, primarily England's in the nineteenth century. Spurred on by its victory over Napoleon, the English government subsequently used the best of what its Royal Navy had to offer in attempt after attempt at finding the route to once again impress upon the world the magnitude of its power and greatness. Even when this extraordinary national enterprise proved to be futile, the mystique of the Northwest Passage persisted into the twentieth century thanks to Amundsen's indefatigable determination, a renaissance in scientific exploration, Canada's desire to assert sovereignty over the region, and the Cold War which made the Arctic a strategic buffer zone between North America and the Soviet Union.

Whether the motivation behind the explorations of the Northwest Passage was a matter of material wealth, or a means to an end for national honor, or part of a continental defence strategy, it was always a focal point for man's undaunted spirit of adventure. In setting out to complete the search that his forefathers started, Amundsen confessed that his desire arose out of a "whisper, clear and insistent: 'If you could do the Northwest Passage!'" His mentor and fellow Norwegian Fridtjof Nansen described the lure as "the power of the unknown over the mind of man." To be sure, the Arctic explorer's ego, greed, and prejudices often made a mess of things, resulting in resentment and bitterness, far-fetched claims, and outright lies, not to mention the loss of human lives. Nevertheless, that undaunted spirit led to many important breakthroughs in science as well as some of the more memorable and inspiring moments in human history. Who, for example, could be anything but moved by the image of John Davis and his men in 1585 dancing alongside a group of Inuit to the melody of a four-piece English chamber orchestra and the beat of aboriginal drums only moments after a very tentative first encounter?

Unfortunately, few Arctic explorers displayed the compassion or sensitivity of John Davis. The approach towards finding the Northwest Passage was essentially an ethnocentric one, guided by the prevailing theories of the time towards a broad range of ideas pertaining to geography, the order of nature, and racial superiority. Never did it occur to Europeans that more than 4000 years had passed since the exploration of the Northwest Passage had been completed along a west-east route by nomadic Indians and Inuit traveling from Siberia and Alaska into the North American interior and polar regions without boats and likely without dog teams. Nor did it occur to the explorers, at least for more than three centuries, to "go native" and adopt the Indian and Inuit ways. In this sense, it is easy to sympathize with the Inuit who saw the European explorers as visitors not discoverers, or with the Dene Indians of the Northwest Territories, who upon being told that Alexander Mackenzie had found the great river that now bears his name, replied that they did not know it had ever been lost.

Today, the entire Arctic has emerged once again as a region of tremendous significance. For some, it represents a huge reservoir of oil, gas and mineral resources or a strategic military zone. To others, it is a splendidly diverse

*An elderly Inuit couple wearing traditional caribou skin clothing.*

ecosystem worthy of protection. To the Dene Indians and the Inuit, who watch as some of these familiar themes unfold largely without their advice or participation, it remains Denendeh and Nunavut—"Land of the People" or "Our Land." Whatever the perspective, the Arctic can no longer be dismissed as a frozen wasteland of interest only to a handful of explorers, traders, missionaries, scientists and aboriginal people, says political scientist Oran Young. It would, however, be "pointless and wasteful," he adds, for those nations with a stake in the region to continue to work at cross-purposes, as has been the case with American and Soviet submarines playing dangerous games of cat-and-mouse below the surface of the Northwest Passage or with Canada and the United States feuding over who controls access to the waterway.

There are, however, signs that a new era of international cooperation in which the Northwest Passage plays a significant role may be at hand. Although the United States and Canada continue to agree to disagree over the Northwest Passage sovereignty question, the Americans have consented to give prior notice to Canada whenever an attempt at navigation is planned. On the other side of the North Pole, the Soviet Union has extended an olive branch to its former foes with the proposal to make the circumpolar Arctic a "zone of peace." In 1987, Soviet president Mikhail Gorbachev pledged a "profound and certain interest in preventing the North of the planet, its Polar and sub-polar regions, and all Northern countries from ever again becoming an arena of war." The challenge, of course, is an enormous one. But there are historical precedents for this kind of cooperation. When the 129 members of the Franklin expedition went missing in 1848, for example, several countries, including British North America (Canada), the United States, France, and Great Britain pledged money, manpower and ships in what turned out to be the biggest search-and-rescue mission in history. In 1882–83, 1932–33 and 1957–58, scientists from all over the world worked together and exchanged information in the International Polar Years. Whether such cooperation can once again be achieved is difficult to determine, but as we head into the twenty-first century, the Northwest Passage is certain to be a litmus test of international relations.

"A North that was poorly known at the outset could not avoid
becoming the target of illusions and prejudices."
—Canadian geographer Louis-Edmond Hamelin, *Canadian Nordicity:
It's Your North Too,* 1979

# 1.
# POLYNYAS
# AND SMOKING HILLS

M ay 13, 1985—On the last leg of our journey, we set off across the sea ice in brilliant sunshine. The weather—calm and −13°F (−25°C)—seems almost balmy compared to the razor-sharp winds and white-out conditions of previous days. Behind us is Bathurst Island, as imposing from afar as it was when we trudged across it; our frozen river passageway—so deep and cavernous when we inched our way along its enormous cliffs—has now been absorbed into the distant, seemingly lifeless monolith rising from the sea.

It had been a struggle crossing Bathurst Island, and the journey over flat ice is no more effortless, at least psychologically. All sense of progress is lost when there are no islands or icebergs to aim for. The continuous sheet of white gives the illusion that you are exercising on a treadmill. And the urban mind, reacting like a computer confronting something beyond the limits of its program, protests. Instinctively, the three of us race ahead on our skis in an attempt to break the monotony. When we finally stop an hour later—out of breath, drenched in sweat, and flush with the kind of euphoria that affects long-distance runners—we are faced with a bewildering apparition on the horizon. There, suspended in midair over the faint outline of Cameron Island to the west, is a flat stretch of land teetering like a saucer on the end of a spoon.

Binoculars pass from one person to the next, and still, even magnified, the image remains airborne, shimmering like a distant car on a hot asphalt highway. The more we push forward, the farther it seems to recede into the distance, until, finally, the mirage fades out of view.

*The exposed bituminous shale of the Smoking Hills near Cape Bathurst in the Western Arctic has been burning spontaneously for 1000 years or more.*

9

*An early nineteenth-century depiction of a mirage by English whaler William Scoresby, Jr.*

North American Indians referred to mirages as Manitou Korso, or "the work of their god." Scientists have adopted the Icelandic term "hillangar" to distinguish the Arctic phenomenon from the more common "desert" mirage, or Fata Morgana. The fact that both are attributable to a logical chain of physical processes makes their occurrence no less fascinating.

Hillangar have the power of "rolling back the horizon" and optically elevating the entire field of view, occasionally for astonishing distances. While a desert mirage represents an image that has been displaced laterally and vertically by unpredictable light paths, the Arctic mirage transposes an image only in the vertical direction. For this phenomenon to occur, certain conditions must be present. A high-pressure system that brings with it prolonged periods of sunshine radiating over cold surfaces—the sea ice on a windless day, for example—is ideal. On such days, usually in early spring, descending cold air from aloft warms as the atmospheric pressure increases. Usually, there's an increase of one degree for every hundred yards of descent. This temperature and air density change causes the air to act like a prism, and so what would normally be a straight line of sight between object and viewer, progressively curves. When this bending of light occurs at a rate that exceeds the earth's curvature, the field of view is optically displaced. The horizon recedes, and the vista that is normally concealed by the horizon, heaves into view.

It has been suggested by at least two scientists that mirages, by facilitating conditions in which the Faeroe Islands could occasionally be seen from the shores of the Shetland Islands, Iceland from the Faeroes, Greenland from Iceland, and North America from Greenland, may have been the source of Viking and Icelandic folklore regarding mysterious lands to the west. These sightings, in turn, the theory goes, gave the Vikings the confidence to set out in search of them, a necessary prerequisite when one considers that the prevailing theories of the time suggested that anyone who ventured too far into the North Atlantic would disappear over the edge of the earth or into treacherous whirlpools, vortices, and sea fences.

Yet, although mirages may have enticed early explorers westward across the North Atlantic, later on they constantly confounded explorers in search of the Northwest Passage and new Arctic lands. In 1818, the British explorer John Ross aborted his voyage through Lancaster Sound on the mistaken premise that there was a range he called the Croker Mountains blocking the way. Had it not been for such junior officers as William Edward Parry contradicting Ross's report following the expedition's return to England, the British Admiralty may well have diverted indefinitely its search for a northwest passage from this most practical of routes.

A mirage may also have caused Storker Storkerson, a member of Vilhjalmur Stefansson's 1913–18 Canadian Arctic expedition, inexplicably to strike out across the south coast of discovered Borden Island to explore the east side instead of the west. With Stefansson, Storkerson was on a mission to find and claim islands within the area of the Northwest Passage on behalf of the Canadian government. Stefansson, who was following closely behind, thought his partner's actions were peculiar. It made much more sense to explore the seaward side while the weather was cold and clear and leave the east coast to later in the season. (When the prevailing, cold northwesterly winds in the High Arctic hit the warm eastern shorelines in spring, a thick fog often forms, making travel difficult.) Storkerson later explained to Stefansson that he had been lured east by the appearance of a land with massive cliffs, which materialized with the lifting of the fog. Surprised, he had studied the image more closely with his binoculars. Even his Inuit companions could not provide an explanation as they had not ventured this far north themselves. So real was the apparition that they had set out to explore it. However, the farther they pushed forward, the farther the land receded into the distance "until finally, without becoming obscured by any fog or mist, it sank beneath the horizon as if it had been some heavenly body setting."

In addition to mirages, the Arctic explorers had to contend with the effects of the landscape on the eye. Crossing the monotonic landscape of a white-out, the sea ice on a cloudy day, or snow-covered land, they often lost all sense of scale and depth of field. The impact on the untrained eye of focusing on a distant object is not unlike that of watching the moon rise in the evening. Against a mountain backdrop or a cityscape of tall buildings, it can appear enormous. But, later on, when it is higher in the sky, away from any point of reference, it seemingly shrinks in size. It is, of course, wholly a matter of perspective since the moon on high is no farther away from the earth than it is on the horizon.

The role of perspective in the search for the Northwest Passage came to mind while I was traveling by snowmobile on the Arctic sea ice in near-whiteout conditions. Finding nothing in the distance to train my eye on, save the backs of my Inuit companions riding ahead of me, I was occasionally given to panic, thinking that they were miles ahead and threatening to disappear from view. If that had happened, I would have been hopelessly lost. In fact, they were only a few hundred feet away. At other times, I was certain that we were climbing and then descending hills. Although I knew that we were moving across the flat sea ice, I frequently found myself leaning back, or to one side of the machine, thinking that I was in danger of overturning.

Confronting similar illusions, it isn't surprising that a number of European explorers changed their intended course or got lost after a sudden storm arose while they were out hunting or exploring on foot. How, then, do the Inuit, without any obvious points of reference, manage to navigate their way through the same white-out conditions with remarkable accuracy? The Inuit are guided by many things, including the wind patterns in the snow and a darkness in the sky that points to a polynya, a patch of open water surrounded by ice that rarely freezes over. Traveling in the Arctic does indeed involve a special way of seeing things, an instinctive way of decoding what strikes those of us from the south as foreign or illusory, that comes only with a long and intimate association with the land.

The British art critic E.H. Gombrich pointed out that every period and every society has its own prejudices in matters of art and taste. And art is a manifestation of the way we look at things, however real or illusory those things may be. Their own illusions and preconceptions about what the New World would be like, as well as nature's illusions, have shaped the way every generation of European explorer has looked at the Arctic and the Northwest Passage, be it through maps, drawings and diaries, or through scientific fact or theory. What evolved over the centuries, in essence, was not simply a search for a short-cut to the Far East in pursuit of fabulous riches, but what Arctic ethnologist Bernard Saladin d'Anglure describes as a pattern of "events, places, prospects, and possibilities" drawn from "an archeology of dreams, myths, beliefs, and facts." In this way, the legacy of the search for the Northwest Passage resembles the mirage—an intriguing mix of myth and reality, science and nescience, truth and error.

This overlapping of myth and reality in the search for the Northwest Passage is best illustrated by the maps and charts used by the explorers. The Zeno chart, first published in 1558, is a good example. Prepared by a Venetian named Niccolò Zeno, it accompanied a narrative of the voyages of his ancestors, Niccolò and Antonio. In 1380, these two brothers were reputed to have sailed into the North Atlantic, where they entered into the service of Zichmni, a northern prince. Some fishermen under Zichmni's rule had apparently visited a place called Estotiland and discovered there an intelligent civilization as well as an abundance of gold and other precious metals. The Zenos set out in search of this land, and over the next two decades reached Iceland and

*British explorers John Ross and William Edward Parry encounter a group of Greenland Inuit in 1818. The contrast in clothing illustrates how ill-prepared these naval officers were in their search for the Northwest Passage.*

Greenland (Engroeneland), an island called Frislanda to the south of them, as well as Estotiland and Drogeo, both of which were purported to be part of North America.

By the nineteenth century, it was generally accepted by historians that these voyages never took place. And today, we regard the narrative and the accompanying chart as mere novelties. However, in 1576, the Zeno chart was a reference for anyone with any inclination to sail into the North Atlantic in search of the Northwest Passage. Both Gerhard Kremer and Abraham Ortelius, two of sixteenth-century Europe's leading cartographers, believed in it. Not surprisingly, so did Martin Frobisher and his navigator James Beare. As a result, both mistook the east coast of Greenland for the apocryphal Frislanda. And, upon discovering "Frobishers Streytes" (Frobisher Bay) and sailing 180 miles (290 km) into it without sighting any land to the west, they were convinced that they had found the passage to the Orient, with the "Meta Incognita" of the New World to the south of them and Asia to the north.

Gerhard Kremer (Gerhardus Mercator) perpetuated this delusion in his famous map of 1569, renowned for its precision and calculation of co-ordinates; it is often cited as one of the great cartographic works of all time. Yet, it not only included many of the fictional features of the Zeno, but also incorporated medieval Scandinavian visions of the North Pole, the most notable being the one of a polar maelstrom swirling around a mountain of rock in the middle of four islands populated by pygmies. A northwest or northern passage, according to Mercator's map, appeared to be practicable only via one of the narrow channels through the lands encircling the Pole.

Given that these early maps reflected a blend of myth and first-hand discovery, it is not surprising that they both served and confused the Northwest Passage explorers who made later use of them. John Davis, in 1585, for example, was, in theory, aware of Frobisher's route, and was no doubt encouraged in his own search for the Northwest Passage by what the earlier explorer had found. But, at the same time, when he sailed down the east coast of Baffin Island he had no idea that he was anywhere near where Frobisher was reported to have landed. In fact, the true location of Frobishers Streytes wasn't conclusively determined until about 300 years later, when American explorer Charles Francis Hall discovered relics from the Frobisher expedition.

Although first-hand discovery by explorers such as Hall usually resulted in the disintegration of myths concerning the location of Arctic lands and the Northwest Passage, it did not necessarily result in immediate enlightenment. There was, points out Canadian geographer William Wonders, a "void that was only gradually filled segment by segment until the overall picture was more or less complete by the end of the Second World War."

In the meantime, it was left up to scientists and explorers themselves to search for the missing segments. As a result, the literature of Arctic exploration is filled with intellectual guesswork that desperately tries to remain faithful to the human aspirations and economic goals of the times without compromising scientific principles. Most notable of the creative scientific thinking that ensued was the notion of an open polar sea to be found in the vicinity of the north geographic pole. The concept was an attractive one to English entrepreneurs seeking passage to the Orient because a polar route appeared to be much shorter than the Spanish or Portuguese passages to the east, around the south tip of Africa.

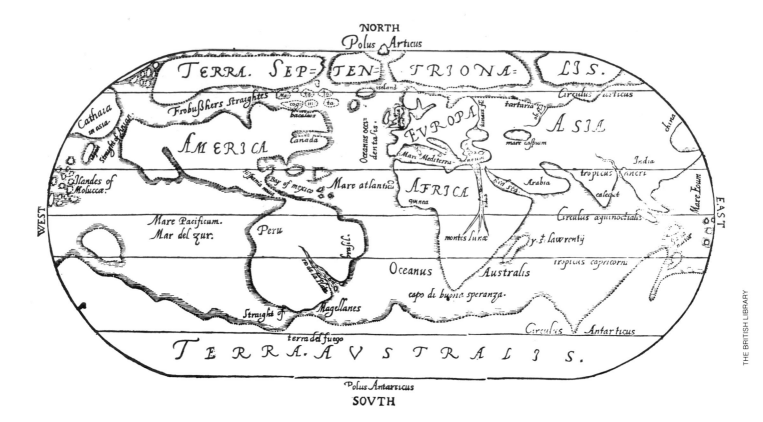

However, the so-called open polar sea was predicated on at least two false notions of climate and oceanography. The first theory, put forth in 1580 by geographer William Bourne, suggested that the long summer days in the North resulted in a corresponding increase in temperature. The second theory, supported by a variety of individuals, including the explorer John Davis, was based on the assumption that ice could be formed only in fresh water. And, so it was thought, the farther one sailed from the freshwater influence of inland rivers, the more ice-free the Arctic Ocean would become.

With the benefit of satellite imaging, we can see today the folly of this way of thinking. Using more primitive scientific tools, some of the geographers of the time did as well. In 1589, for example, Thomas Blundeville openly challenged Bourne's concept by asking "what heat can the Sunne yeelde to that place above whose horizon he is never elevated more than 23 degrees and a halfe, a verie cold winterlie heat God wotte." So appealing was the notion of an open polar sea to the aspirations of Arctic explorers, though, that a number of them, including Constantine Phipps (1773), David Buchan (1818), William Penny (1850–51), Elisha Kent Kane (1853–55), and Isaac Hayes (1860–61) headed off on their respective journeys with the idea of an open polar sea planted firmly in their minds. Both Penny and Hayes returned from their voyages convinced that they had indeed found it. What they had in fact encountered were polynyas; in Penny's case, the Dundas Island polynya; in Hayes's, the huge North Water.

Although it was not the hoped for open polar sea, the North Water played an important role in the search for the Northwest Passage. This open body of water links the Atlantic and Arctic oceans and was used by Northwest Passage explorers to reach Lancaster Sound and by whalers to get to their "fishing grounds." Given the climatic conditions of the area, there was, and still is, every reason to assume that this body of water should freeze over in winter.

*World map illustrating Martin Frobisher's voyages, published in 1578.*

The fact that it doesn't, nineteenth-century scientists logically attributed to some mechanic of oceanography—the saltiness of the water or the twenty-four hours of summer sunlight. (Later scientists found that it was due to a combination of factors involving tides, currents, winds, and ocean upwellings.)

If polynyas like the North Water existed, reasoned the scientists and explorers, why not an open polar sea closer to the Pole? When Elisha Kent Kane sailed into the North Water in 1853 in search of the missing Franklin expedition, one of the first things that he noticed was ice drifting southward. Deducing that this was what kept the North Water open, he was puzzled to find that, farther north, the flow of ice ended. He speculated that, even farther north, there was no ice in the waters to drift southward. In 1861, the great pioneering oceanographer Matthew Fontaine Maury lent credence to Kane's theory. After studying the over-winter drifts of the *Rescue* and *Advance* in 1850–51, and the *Fox* in 1857–58—Maury found that each one of them had drifted south with the ice. At the same time, however, those aboard the vessels reported a northward drift of large deep-draft icebergs against the south-flowing current. From these observations, Maury concluded that there was a warm subsurface current moving northward that lay below a surface current heading in the opposite direction. This warm current, he believed, eventually rose to the surface in an open polar sea. It wasn't until 1928, after two expeditions to the North Water, that the notion of the open polar sea was scientifically and conclusively dismissed.

Illusions about the Arctic and a northwest passage evolved as much out of the aesthetic mind as they did from the maps and scientific views of the time. In the case of the eighteenth- and nineteenth- century British explorers, it was the perceptual view of the landscape that was most pervasive, a view in which all nature was described in terms of either the Sublime or the Picturesque. The Sublime, to the British of this era, referred to those aspects of nature that defied description or the imagination—the open prairie, the wild mountain peak, the swirling storm.

Looking at landscape paintings by artists such as J.M.W. Turner, the viewer feels small and overwhelmed in the face of powers that he cannot control. It is a fantastic world in which nature is portrayed in the context of a ghastly chaos unfolding, but one that exudes "resplendent beauty," and "dazzling pageantry" at the same time. The Picturesque, on the other hand, looked at nature "as a pleasing setting for idyllic scenes." Picturesque painters like Claude Lorrain positioned the foreground and background at about the same height, with the middle ground in a sunken position. The main idea, consciously or unconsciously, was to look down on nature to find views that could be controlled.

The Arctic—vast, mysterious, terrible, and beautiful—was anything but controllable. As such, it provided the perfect backdrop for British responses to the Sublime. Samuel Taylor Coleridge's popular "The Rime of the Ancient Mariner" was, along with Mary Shelley's *Frankenstein*, one of the literary works that helped shape the Victorian view of the polar world. Both, coincidentally, appeared in print only months before the Admiralty's first Victorian-era ships reached the Arctic in 1818. In Coleridge's poem, south polar scenes are depicted, but the inspiration was almost certainly Arctic in origin, and many Arctic explorers quoted it in their narratives. The voyagers in his poem encounter the albatross in this sublime landscape where "through the drifts the snowy cliffs" no living thing was to be seen. Although the albatross proves to be a good omen, and the ship is delivered by winds back to more familiar seas, the Ancient Mariner kills it with a cross-bow. Arctic historian and traveler Chauncey Loomis suggests that the thematic conclusion, which offers that "the dear God who loveth us/He made and loveth all," anticipates the Victorian response to the Arctic by making it an environment that provoked theological speculation. Like the voyagers in Coleridge's poem, the explorers themselves were frequently led to wonder about a God who doesn't discriminate between the terrible and the beautiful. Loomis also might have added that many of the explorers also counted on divine power to will the "course and might of all elemental forces" which "no earthly power could overcome."

Although both the Picturesque and the Sublime figured prominently in the search for the Northwest Passage, it was the Sublime Arctic that prevailed in a literary sense and in the minds of the public during the most intense period of British exploration between 1818 and 1859. Yet the Admiralty and the explorers often ignored or pushed aside the dangers that stood before them. Their tendency was to portray the Arctic in terms of the Picturesque even when the reality did not merit it. While it predates the Victorian era, the anonymous narrative of Constantine Phipps' 1773 voyage is a typical example. In what should have been a harrowing scene after their ship became trapped in the ice, the journalist on board one of the expedition ships depicts the situation in much the same way that an Englishman might have described a casual stroll in the countryside. The air was "perfectly serene, and the weather moderate," he writes, "…the fishes seemed to enjoy the temperature, and to express it by their sporting. The whales have been spouting their fountains towards the skies, and the fin fish follow their example…the whole prospect in short was more pleasing and picturesque than they yet beheld in this remote region. The very ice in which they were beset looked beautiful, and put forth a thousand glittering forms, and the tops of the mountains, which they could see like sparkling gems at a vast distance had the appearance of so many silver stars illuminating a new firmament."

The tendency of the British explorers to romanticize the Arctic landscape at the most inappropriate times struck me when I first saw the Smoking Hills in the western Arctic. Here, along 20 miles (30 km) of cliffs near Cape Bathurst, are pockets of exposed bituminous shale that have been burning spontaneously for 1000 years or more. The smoke consists of sulphur dioxide, sulphuric acid aerosol, and steam, and is carried by the wind over the tundra or Franklin Bay. The preconception I had of them from the narrative of Robert McClure, who, in 1850, set out in search of the missing Franklin expedition via the Bering Sea, was one of "volcanoes, about fifty feet above water and situated on an old land-slip, not unlike the undercliff of the Isle of Wight." The *Investigator*'s artist, Samuel Gurney Cresswell, painted a single spiral of thick smoke rising gently from the cliff-side at the edge of a placid sea.

The environmental reality, however, conveys something quite different. While I was there, the strong winds that blow in from the Beaufort Sea whipped up whitecaps that came crashing in against the eroded cliffs. The smoke smoldered from several sources; dramatically in some instances, inconsequentially in others. The smell of sulphur was at times overwhelming, and the path we took through the burned mounds on the beaches was muddy, ash-filled and precarious.

This kind of metaphorical taming of the Arctic became the norm in the published narratives of the commanders and in the paintings of the British expedition artists. In an essay touching on this subject, literary critic I.S. MacLaren illustrates how the British explorers of the Franklin era were often misled (and misled others in the process) by their own illusions about the Arctic landscape. These depictions, he says, tending as they did to digress from environmental reality in order to fit into the more familiar schemata of English landscape taste of the time, fortified British optimism and morale sufficiently to see the search for Franklin to a successful conclusion. However, they also produced disastrous consequences for many of the searchers.

MacLaren points to one of the most dramatic examples, involving Franklin himself on his 1819–22 overland journey to the Arctic coast in search of a northwest passage. In this case, it was the choice of encampment that he, John Richardson, Robert Hood, and George Back made when they reached their wintering site at Fort Enterprise. From the writings of three of them, it appears that the decision was made with a view to the Picturesque. "We could not have selected a more convenient or beautiful spot," wrote Richardson to his mother. "The surrounding country is finely varied by hill and dale and interspersed with numerous lakes connected by small streams." The "beauty of the situation," Hood noted in his diary, "far exceeded our most sanguine expectations.... The sole remaining characteristic of the country we had lately traversed, was a gloomy barrier of sterile hills in front, parallel to the river, which only served to heighten the enjoyment of our retreat, by reminding us of the misery which we had escaped."

Again, my own visit to the site resulted in a completely different impression. What struck me as peculiar was why anyone would have built a shelter so exposed to the elements and so far removed from food sources when such were readily available at one of the nearby large lakes. This decision, of course, came back to haunt Richardson and Franklin when they returned to the encampment after a summer's trek along the Arctic coast. Close to death from starvation, neither they nor their companions could muster the strength to walk down to the lake to fish.

George Back must have learned this lesson well when, in 1833, he set off in search of John Ross, who, although shunned by the British Admiralty over the Croker Mountain affair, had managed to win the support of gin merchant Felix Booth for a second voyage in 1829. Ross and his crew had been missing for nearly four years, and Back was appointed to find them by way of an overland journey via Great Slave Lake and the Great Fish River. Back's first winter was spent at a fort he had built at the east end of Great Slave. But, unlike Fort Enterprise, Fort Reliance was nestled in a forest close to the mouth of the Lockhart River. (The stone chimneys and fireplaces, which were a feature of the four separate rooms leading into a spacious hall, still stand today.) By any standard other than the Picturesque, it was a wise choice of sites. Nevertheless, Back was so conditioned to the Picturesque point of view that he was unable or unwilling to depict the site in any other way. "The site of our intended dwelling," he wrote, "was a level bank of gravel and sand, covered with reindeer moss, shrubs, and trees, and looking more like a park than part of an American forest." And, in describing the daily activities, he wrote, "it was an animated scene; and, set off as it was by the white tents and smoky leather lodges, contrasting with the mountains and green woods, it was picturesque as

*A detail from* Building Fort Enterprise on the Winter River, Northwest Territories, *painted by Robert Hood in 1820.*

well as interesting." (A park it is not, nor are there mountains of any kind in the vicinity.)

Traveling with illusions of the Picturesque no doubt had a generous effect on the morale of explorers like Back and his colleagues. It made them comfortable with their environment because they were often ignorant of the dangers that loomed over them, like someone who knows nothing of bears who hikes with fish bait through grizzly bear country. At the same time, such illusions were bound to bring misfortune, just as they did on Franklin's first overland journey. Between 1818 and 1859, the British explorers had their share of misfortunes. But instead of rethinking their perceptual schemata or their approach to travel in the Arctic world, they simply became more tenacious in their old ways. Doubts did overcome those like James Clark Ross who in September 1831 asked himself whether there is "anyone who loves the sight of ice and snow? I imagine now, that I always doubted this." Yet even Ross, faced with a third winter in the Arctic, quickly regained his composure by reassuring himself that "this also is Picturesque, I admit, as are the frozen summits of the Alps...and they are not the less beautiful that they are." Failure, so long as it did not result in the extraordinary loss of British lives, simply heightened the appeal of the Sublime. Here, in effect, was nature that challenged British strength and courage and imagination.

It was only when the Admiralty suspected that Franklin and his men had met with a horrible demise that the explorers began to sense that the snow and ice in a Picturesque landscape painting were not, as I.S. MacLaren suggests, the same as snow and ice that beset "a scurvy-ridden crew of incarcerated sojourners at the greatest odds with the surrounding environment." When, for example, H.M.S. *Investigator* encountered pack ice pushing southward through Prince of Wales Strait in 1851, Alexander Armstrong, the expedition's surgeon/naturalist, concluded that "no earthly means of any magnitude or power, aided by all the best appliances of art, and guided by the judgment, ingenuity, and best energies of man, could avail in the slightest degree, in surmounting the overwhelming obstacles, which, on these occasions, opposed our progress." Divine intervention, he believed, was all that could be counted on. William Kennedy, who survived a particularly harsh winter in 1851–52 searching for Franklin, wondered whether the Arctic was part of God's domain at all. At one point in his narrative, he sees himself and his crew sledging across the Arctic like the fallen angels of John Milton's *Paradise Lost*.

In time, the Picturesque eye looked away and the voice of the Sublime, which depended on maintaining a safe distance from nature's ominous powers, fell silent. The movement of the pack ice and the unfamiliar qualities of the Arctic environment simply overwhelmed or confused the explorers. Frustrated by their powerlessness, the shortcomings of their own perceptual schemata, and the failure to find either Franklin or the Northwest Passage, the British eventually dismissed the Arctic as a bleak and uninhabitable land—so sterile in some places that even the Eskimo were forced to desert it. And so by 1859, when Leopold McClintock had returned to England with confirmation of Franklin's demise, the search for the Northwest Passage was all but abandoned.

Another half century would pass before anyone seriously challenged this bleak view of the Arctic. The most famous of them was Vilhjalmur Stefansson, a Canadian-born American explorer who was involved in three remarkable

*George Back's 1833–34 overland expedition sledging across Lake Aylmer at 3 a.m.*

Arctic expeditions between 1903 and 1918, the final one of which took five and a half years. A brilliant but egotistical man—some suggested he was an egomaniac—Stefansson boasted that he could have lived in the Arctic fifteen and a half years as easily as five and half. In one of his many books, this one appropriately named *The Friendly Arctic*, he outlines his approach to polar travel, first by summarizing "the Four Stages of Arctic Exploration," then by debunking popular conceptions about the Arctic world.

European explorers first traveled to the Arctic with the firm belief that they could not survive a winter, Stefansson suggested. Experience, however, proved that this was possible and eventually preferable because traversing on foot over snow and ice was often easier than stumbling over wet tundra or steering ships through ice-infested waters in summer and autumn.

Britain's folly, according to Stefansson, was in putting too much faith in "a North that never was." The explorers, he reasoned, were very much like the later immigrants who had come to the American prairies from a forested or mountainous country. In their minds, the prairie landscape was desolate and dreary because they missed what was familiar to them. Consequently, they "strained" their vocabulary to find a way to describe what they did not know. Stefansson could forgive the British for having done the same thing. What he really objected to was the fact that experience hadn't taught them anything and that they would, in the end, resort to a pseudo-scientific argument to dismiss the Arctic as bleak and lifeless and suggest that every voyage made was done at great risk, "to expand the horizon of man's knowledge." This, he saw, as a fraudulent means of justifying how 129 of Britain's finest men could have perished. If the "idea of the barrenness could have been shed," he said, "there would have been no Franklin tragedy or Franklin search. Franklin's men would not have starved to death, as we now know they did, in a region where game is abundant."

Stefansson's *Friendly Arctic* was as much a rebellion against the British view of the Arctic as it was his own personal, but not altogether unique vision. The so-called "barren ground" was in his mind "a vast pasture," or "Northern prairie" out of which billions of tons of edible vegetation went to waste yearly. He envisioned the day when tens of thousands of domesticated reindeer and muskoxen would inhabit huge game ranches in the Far North to help feed an expanding population. He also predicted that the "lifeless Arctic sea" would become a "Polar Mediterranean," because it "contains about as much life to the cubic mile of water as any other sea."

Recognizing the lush character or the "friendly" nature of the Arctic was not as original an idea as Stefansson often led people to believe. When the naturalist Ernest Thompson Seton traveled to the Far North by canoe in 1909, for example, he was so impressed with the lushness of the landscape that he dubbed the tundra "The Arctic Prairie." Fridtjof Nansen himself hinted at feeling ashamed for promulgating the popular view that suffering through a long winter night was indispensable to an exciting Arctic expedition. And Roald Amundsen, while over-wintering at Gjoa Haven on King William Island in 1903–04, said, "it is one of the most beautiful and lovely spots on the American north coast," an "Arctic Eden" that was teeming with wildlife and food resources.

Amundsen, however, regarded Stefansson's view of the Arctic world as dangerous and distorted. He even offered to stake his reputation as an explorer on a wager that Stefansson would be dead in eight days if he attempted to live on the polar ice without supplies. It was a wager, however, that he eventually lost, at least in the public arena. Towards the end of his exploration years, prospective investors turned him away, suggesting that he live off the land. "What really irked Amundsen," suggests one of his biographers, "was the threat the 'friendly Arctic' theory posed to fund-raising."

Stefansson's vision, however, was just as warped by perceptual prejudices as were those of the British. Growing up on the American prairie, he had developed a perspective rooted in economics. Based on the eighteenth century agrarian myth, this outlook derived largely from John Locke's notion that land was the common stock of all society, which every man has a right to exploit.

Many American expansionists used the agrarian myth as the basis for their strategy of continental development, whether in relation to ranching, planting wheat, or mining coal. The unsettled lands of the West in the late nineteenth century were seen as a means of guaranteeing the "preponderance of the yeoman." But, by the turn of the century, once the West was largely filled, many, like Stefansson, started looking north to Alaska and beyond. "We have not come to the northward limit of commercial progress," Stefansson wrote in outlining his vision. "There was a pause but no stop to the westward course of empire until we came to the place where East is West. In that sense only is there a northward limit to progress.... There is no boundary beyond which productive enterprise cannot go till North meets North on the opposite shores of the Arctic Ocean as East has met West on the Pacific."

Stefansson's view of the Arctic, as outlined in *The Friendly Arctic* and *The Northward Course of Empire*, was thus largely an extension of the American frontier mentality to include the Arctic world. In his proposals, he was just as guilty as were the British of taming the Arctic. Yet, Stefansson was shrewd enough to understand that his was a valid view only if it could be shown that the Arctic was worthy of exploitation and settlement. And that, to him, meant undoing the "literary North" as the world knew it at the turn of the century.

Stefansson went to extremes to drive home his argument, referring to muskoxen as "cattle" or "sheep-cow" at one point, and then proposing that the government officially refer to them as "ovibos" to help dispel the false notion that the meat had a musky flavor. The Arctic lands, he believed, could produce as much meat per acre as those stock lands of the south that are too dry for cereal crops. One need only look at the "fat" and "healthy" Inuit, Stefansson often suggested, to see what a lush and resource-rich place the Arctic really was.

The only weak link in the equation, at least in Stefansson's mind, was in the apparent waning of the frontier spirit in the United States and the unwillingness of the Canadian government to truly embrace it. "All over our 'civilized' world," he complained, "is seen a tendency of the land folk to crowd into the cities.... It is said that we are becoming a weakened and softened nation, not only because the frontier is not here any longer to struggle with, but also because we shrink increasingly from any struggle with Nature." "If Canada were to keep pace with the Americans," he added, it "must recognize the productivity and habitability of all her territories."

Stefansson worked so hard to package everything into this "friendly" vision of the Arctic world and into his whole notion of a "northward course of empire" that he rejected all the evidence around him that pointed to the contrary. The tragic sinking of the *Karluk*, a ship that he claimed was worthy of Arctic travel, was but one example. So was the failure of a commercial reindeer operation that he helped finance and promote on Baffin Island. And while there were "fat" and "healthy" Inuit, as he suggested, these same people were often victims of famines that frequently wiped out entire nomadic groups. All it took was a change in the migration paths of the caribou or the overhunting of one group of animals. Certainly, marine mammals were relatively abundant in his "Mediterranean of the Arctic," but it was also not uncommon for a particularly cold and windy season in one part of the Arctic to create extremely heavy ice conditions that would drive most of them away.

For a country like Canada that had inherited the Arctic Archipelago and the Northwest Passage from Great Britain in July 1880, Stefansson's overly optimistic notion of northern development was both exciting and daunting. In his introduction to *The Friendly Arctic*, Canadian Prime Minister Robert Borden seemed prepared in 1921 to follow through on Stefansson's theories of settlement and development of the North. "Who would venture to declare that they may not be justified as fully as his [Stefansson's] confidence in the Beaufort Sea? Men still living can remember that at first the great prairie provinces of Canada were regarded as unfit for human habitation. Once it was firmly held that railroads could not be operated in Canada during the winter." However, the Canadian government had neither the economic resources nor the political wherewithal to come to terms with how it would direct this northward course of empire while, at the same time, controlling the activities of other countries that had historical and economic roots there. Canadian geographer Louis-Edmond Hamelin describes the dilemma that Canada found itself in as one of "conflicting and mutually regulating emotions: mirages and disappointments" or double illusions. Attractive mirages gave rise to the notion that the North represented Canada's economic and spiritual future. These were constantly being tempered by disappointments, which mostly stemmed from the failure of get-rich-quick schemes.

In fact, one can look at almost any aspect of Canadian policy and public concern relating to the Northwest Passage and the Arctic Archipelago in a more modern context and find the double illusion operating in full force. At the turn of the century, Prime Minister Wilfrid Laurier sent out Joseph-Elzéar

NATIONAL MUSEUMS OF CANADA

*Vilhjalmur Stefansson, carrying a rifle and pike, hauls a seal along the ice during the Canadian Arctic expedition of 1913–18.*

Bernier and others to control the activities of the whalers, all the while fretting that the whalers would take offence at paying customs duties. Through the Second World War and the Cold War years of the 1950s, there was a need to co-operate with the United States in defending the North American continent, as well as a corresponding need, as political scientist Franklyn Griffiths points out, to "defend against help" when the Americans started taking too much control. In the 1960s, and again in the 1980s, the Canadian public was outraged over the voyages of two U.S. ships, the *Manhattan* and *Polar Sea*, because they had sailed through the Northwest Passage without seeking Canadian permission. Both incidents precipitated government action to strengthen Canadian sovereignty over the Northwest Passage, but then faded into the background, as many government initiatives do, once public attention died down. Again, as Griffiths points out, "myth mixes with reality to produce frequently exaggerated attachments and aversions in the domestic and international outlook of a people that has yet to come to grips with the north."

For more than 500 years, the Arctic sublime of the Northwest Passage has enticed and repelled, gratified and imperiled generations of explorers, scientists and entrepreneurs. It has been the backdrop to a reckless struggle with nature that began with an understandable desire to find a commercially viable passage to the Orient and ended in a tragic pursuit engineered to serve the ego of a nation more than anything else. Under Canadian stewardship, the fascination continues, but subject to the roller-coaster moods of public opinion just as it was during the long search for the Passage.

*A dead beached beluga whale on the tidal flats in Cunningham Inlet, Somerset Island.*

*In addition to the early explorers, whaling and fishing fleets frequented the northern waters. This illustration appears in a 1650 account of Jens Munk's voyage.*

*Breakup in mid-July. Only a day before this photograph was taken, this was a 10-ft (3-m) thick sheet of ice. Within a few days all the ice may disintegrate with the right weather conditions.*

# WATER AND ICE

*The shoreline of Eclipse Sound with Bylot Island in the distance.*

"A single trial is often sufficient for satisfying us as to the truth of a disputed point, but in this instance [the search for the Northwest Passage], though nearly an hundred trials have been made, the problem is still considered unresolved."
— WILLIAM SCORESBY, JR., ARCTIC WHALER AND SCIENTIST, 1820

# 2.

# META INCOGNITA:
# EARLY VOYAGES

---

*A Baffin Bay iceberg in spring melt. The bay was discovered in 1615 by Robert Bylot and named for his commander, William Baffin.*

A
pril 21, 1989—We had enjoyed a good part of our day in Penny Strait, drilling holes in the sea ice to listen to the spooky, descending trills of bearded seals and the bell-knock codas of male walruses in the polynya nearby. (While searching for a mate, the male walrus makes a series of knocking sounds by clicking its tongue against the roof of its mouth. The final movement of the composition ends with a bell-knock, similar to that of a church bell.) Now it was time to head back to Dundas Island where my scientist companions intended to remain while I flew by helicopter to Resolute, about 100 miles (160 km) to the south. It was snowing hard when we said our goodbyes. The temperature had plummeted, and the distant, stormy sky was billowing with violet-blues and dark greys more commonly associated with a boreal-forest fire. I kept my fears about the weather to myself, hoping that the pilot would utter them first. He didn't. Five minutes after take-off, we were in the thick of a great deal of soupy moisture, and I was feeling a rush of certainty that it was time to turn back.

For whatever reason, the pilot surrendered himself to the situation, turned his back on the security of the coastline, and directed the helicopter out over the invisible mass of broken ice and open sea in the hope of making it to the north coast of Cornwallis Island. It's a daredevil strategy that sometimes works. Local fog along a coast often thins out past the open water. Not in this case. I knew we were in trouble when the helicopter slowed to a crawl, and the engine, shaking perceptibly, was working hard not to carry the machine any faster. "There's a 400-foot-high point of land somewhere ahead of us." The pilot's voice on the intercom sounded anxious. "If you see anything at all, let me know."

Outside our Plexiglas bubble, just 300 feet (90 m) above the surface, there was nothing to see. The world was uniformly daubed by the same grey-white brushstroke. These are critical times for a pilot, and terrifying ones for a passenger, when up and down mean nothing and when safety depends entirely on the accuracy of the helicopter's instruments. Even the most experienced pilots become disoriented flying blind. Occasionally they panic, distrust what their instruments are telling them, and rely instead on their own instincts. When this happens, they may crash the machine into the ground or against a cliff—like the one we were heading for.

I pressed the helicopter's intercom button and suggested we look for a spot to set down until the weather cleared. The pilot didn't answer, then cast a worried glance towards me and asked if I had said something. "Are you okay?" I asked, taking a different approach. He nodded and said, "I can't see a damn thing!" Ironically, his words had a calming effect. Fear, I've always felt, signals a healthy sense of reality. Moments later, that reality loomed into view as the only significant rise on what is a remarkably flat northern coastline suddenly materialized in the fog. The pilot, once again in full control, expertly raised the machine straight up to clear it, and then, seeing that attempting passage over the land was as futile as it had been over the sea, carefully set the machine down.

*Nineteenth-century explorer George Back's watercolor of an enormous iceberg, a ship and walrus near the entrance to Hudson Strait.*

Sitting there, marooned on the northwest coast of Cornwallis Island in spite of the best navigational tools the twentieth century could offer, I was reminded of a story told by Captain Thomas C. Pullen, a veteran of modern Arctic marine operations. It was about what we think is possible in tackling the Northwest Passage today and what is, indeed, practical. At the time, Pullen had just returned from a remarkable Arctic operation in which a $50 million Canadian-built processing plant for lead and zinc ores was towed from Trois-Rivières, Quebec, to a mine on Little Cornwallis Island, about 100 miles (160 km) from where our helicopter was stranded. Prior to the event, experts and planners had boasted about how "marvelous" the communications and how "splendid" the ice and weather forecasts would be. During the actual tow, however, sunspot activity frequently disrupted radio communications, while the facsimile receiver disgorged a succession of distorted or illegible weather maps. Furthermore, the towing vessel encountered heavy ice where officials had reported ice-free conditions.

With this story in mind, I walked through the soft glow of fog and snow crystals and tried to imagine what it was like for early explorers who, without the aid of any of our twentieth-century technology, set out in small barks and traveled for fifty or sixty days against the prevailing westerlies towards an unknown land. Their voyages had more to do with what was thought possible than with faith in what was practical, for not only were they without the means to determine longitude, they were often unable to use the stars as navigational aids because of long days and cloud cover.

There can be no minimizing the risk associated with these early searches for a passage to the Orient; John Cabot's failure to return from his second voyage in 1498 followed by the failure of both Gaspar Corte-Real in 1501 and his brother Miguel in 1502 attest to that. Others, to be sure, were more successful later on, managing to sail as far as Baffin Bay or Hudson Bay. But they also paid a high price. There, in the Arctic seas, even seasoned sailors watched with "hideous fascination" as massive, moving floes, the likes of which they had never imagined, tossed great blocks of ice weighing 50 tons (45 400 kg) or more on top of one another, crushing all hope of pushing further ahead. Those whose vessels became trapped between floes found their ships squeezed so tightly that the tarred oakum squirted out of the seams. An alarming number of ships crumbled under the terrific strain and sank. Others sailed home with scurvy-weakened men, some with their legs or feet amputated as a result of frost-bite—all with tales of hardship that would seem certain to deter even the bravest from following in their wake.

And yet the high stakes in finding a northwest passage were evidently sufficient to conquer the worst fears of those who did contemplate searching for it, and to keep alive the prospects that its discovery was, in fact, possible. For many of the ships' captains and their crews, finding the "most richest londes and ilondes in the worlde, for all the golde, spices, aromatikes, and pretiose stones," guaranteed not only untold wealth, but also fame. In that desire to achieve wealth and immortality, the crudity of navigation, the hunger, the cold, and the sickness, were, as remarkable as it might seem today, more troublesome than they were deterring.

Although the Dutch, Spanish, Portuguese, and Danes participated in this early search for a northerly passage to the Orient, it was Britain that eventually came to dominate it, not so much by choice as by necessity and proximity to the North. During the 1490s, Portugal and Spain, with their superior fleets, were both well on their way to controlling the southern passages round the tips of Africa and South America. The Turks had consolidated their hold on the overland route through the Mediterranean and south-central Asia. The only secure passages left for an agricultural country like England, with its neophyte naval ambitions, were to the west, the north, the northwest, or the northeast —passages that it continued to pursue with varying degrees of interest for the next 350 years.

It would be wrong to assume that these early searches arose solely out of a new and sudden faith in the existence of a northwest passage. In reality, they were a logical continuation of Arctic water explorations made by the likes of Pytheas of Massilia, the Greek explorer who sailed to Britain and Iceland in the fourth century; Saint Brendan and fourteen other Irish monks who reputedly ventured off into the North Atlantic in their leather-covered currachs in the sixth century; and numerous Viking ships thereafter. There is nothing to suggest that these early explorers had any thought of a passage to the East in mind.

What these early voyages did, in fact, do for future Northwest Passage seekers was contribute to the evolving geographical understanding of Arctic waters and how they could be navigated. Pytheas's observations on the position of the stars, the differing length of days and nights, and the connection between the tides and the moon, for example, laid the foundation for marine navigation and future representations of the earth. Although the accounts of Saint Brendan's voyages were primarily allegorical, the places he depicted bear an uncanny resemblance to the Shetlands, the Faeroe Islands, and Iceland, and fueled myths and folklore that inspired future Northwest Passage explorers to search out land masses.

If, indeed, it was the appearance of these mirages that gave the early Viking explorers the gumption to make sail from places like the Shetlands to the Faeroe Islands, from the Faeroes to Iceland, and from Iceland to Greenland and North America, then John Cabot's preparatory voyages in the decade prior to his famous expedition in 1497 make sense. Not much is known about these early efforts, but Cabot, it seems, spent a good deal of time searching for islands that were reported to lie off the western coast of Europe. While the existence of these was based more on folklore than on fact, Cabot had evidently come to believe, as the Vikings had probably done hundreds of years earlier, that he could use these islands as stopover points on his journey to the Orient. In 1493, however, he abandoned the search for the mysterious islands after receiving news that Christopher Columbus, a Genoese sailor like himself, had reached the East by sailing west from Spain.

There was never, of course, any indication that Cabot was specifically looking for a northwest passage as we know it, especially in light of his firm belief that the New World he reached (Cape Breton Island was probably his first landing) was part of northeast Asia. The beginnings of that search must be credited to his son Sebastian. The younger Cabot was an opportunist who was not above playing one country off against another for his services, but just how experienced and knowledgeable he was when it came to northwest navigation is controversial. There is some evidence to suggest that he had accompanied his father on previous expeditions and had probably set off on his own in 1504 with two ships belonging to British merchants. His most important voyage, though, seems to have occurred in 1508 or 1509, when he sailed with two ships and 300 men supplied by King Henry VII. Although, for a time, there was speculation that he fabricated this voyage, new evidence suggests that his vessels sailed through Hudson Strait and into Hudson Bay.

Unfortunately for Cabot, it was a different England that he returned to in 1509. The new king, Henry VIII, had no immediate desire to continue financing the search that his father had begun. The explorer wisely returned to Spain, apparently keeping to himself most of the details of his Northwest discoveries. What happened to him for the next decade remains largely a mystery, although we do know that in 1521 he returned to England to drum up support for another voyage. This time, however, neither the Merchant Adventurers of London that he helped to establish nor the Drapers Company was willing to put up the investment, either because they thought his plan too dangerous or because they weren't convinced by his claims to have discovered previously a northwest passage. Whatever the reason, nothing came of the proposal, and Cabot once again slipped into the background, only to emerge years later as a member of the Muscovy Company of merchants, which, ironically, devoted most of its attention to the search for a northeast passage around Eurasia.

In the meantime, not everyone had given up hope of enlisting the support of the king in a search for a passage to the Orient. Among the most important of the supplicants was Robert Thorne, the son and nephew of the two men who had sponsored Cabot's earlier expedition in 1504. Once a mayor of the port city of Bristol, Thorne owed his business successes to entrepreneurial endeavors in Spain. It was a situation he regarded as not entirely satisfactory. He found no solace in seeing fleet after Spanish fleet unloading valuable Oriental and Indian cargoes while his own countrymen watched from the shore. "To discover the planet, mankind would have to be liberated from ancient hopes and fears, and open the gateways of experience," he wrote in 1527 in support of the new spirit of the Renaissance. "The largest dimensions of space, the continents and the oceans, were only slowly revealed. The West proved a vantage point, and for most of history the West would be the discoverer. The first reaches from the West to another half of the planet came from laborious and lonely overland travelers. But the full extent of the planet could be glimpsed only by organized communities of adventure on the sea, which became a highway to grand surprises."

While the expeditions of Pytheas and the Vikings contributed to Thorne's belief that the Arctic waters could become England's highway to the Orient, it was two earlier journeys, by Marco Polo and Ferdinand Magellan, that inspired it. After Polo's overland travels to the Orient between 1271 and 1295, European merchants had begun to seek out ways to bring the spices and silks of Zipangu or Japan to the West.

Magellan's three-year voyage around the world between 1519 and 1522 by way of South America's Cape Horn showed how it could be done without having to pay tariffs or confront the hostile Turks along the way. The voyage was also important in another, more significant sense. By demonstrating that the world's oceans were one, it established and set into motion what the American historian Stephen J. Pyne describes as a process of discovery. Traditional exploratory techniques and interpretive systems essentially broke down from then on, he explains. "The world ocean could not be assimilated by a simple elaboration of piloting skills and portolan charts developed for the Mediterranean and the Baltic-North seas. There were problems of scale that could not be solved through a simple enlargement, but that demanded new principles of organization."

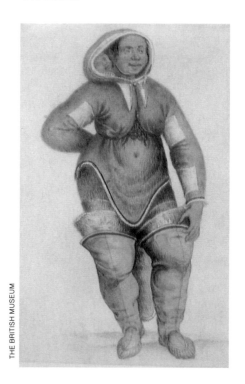

*Sixteenth-century English artist John White produced these drawings of an Inuit man and woman.*

Robert Thorne was one of the few individuals of his time who comprehended the enormity of the challenge. He realized that if a passage to the Orient were to be found, it would require the backing of a nation and the best that science could offer. In essence, exploration needed to become an institutionalized endeavor. His initial strategy, therefore, was to enlist the support of the King. In a letter to Henry VIII in 1531, Thorne argued that discovery of a polar route would not only provide England with peaceful access to the Orient, but also give it the advantage over its Spanish and Portuguese rivals as the passage was 2000 leagues (10 000 km) shorter than one around Africa or South America. To prove his point, he drew on the expertise of cartographers and produced a map of the world, believed to be the first drawn by an Englishman.

Henry VIII was never very enthusiastic about the prospects of finding a northwest or polar passage, so nothing of any import arose out of Thorne's proposal. But the idea continued to intrigue Englishmen after Thorne died in 1532. Robert Barlow, Thorne's friend and fellow entrepreneur, for example, suggested that even failure to find the polar passage could be compensated by the sale of English woolens to the inhabitants of Iceland and Greenland. Henry VIII initially gave his approval. But a last-minute squabble with the pilot over how much he would be paid scuttled the planned expedition.

It was Mercator's map of 1569 that ultimately discouraged interest in the polar route, at least temporarily. With its menacing whirlpools and narrow channels that flowed into a body of water around a rock at the North Pole, the prospects of successful navigation appeared to be daunting. As a consequence, interest over the next century turned towards a northwest passage around the New World which Mercator on his map had separated from Asia, and for a shorter period, towards the northeast around Eurasia.

Europe's initial search for the Northeast Passage had, in fact, already begun rather inauspiciously with Sebastian Cabot's dispatch of three ships in 1553 under the command of Sir Hugh Willoughby. As governor of what eventually came to be known as the Muscovy Company, the younger Cabot banked on his own and his father's reputation to persuade his fellow entrepreneurs to provide the financial backing for the expedition. But Willoughby's tale is as tragic as any in the chronicles of Arctic exploration. His lead-sheathed ships, designed to protect the hulls against tropical worms, never came close to being tested by warm waters. A vicious storm along the Norwegian coast separated them, leaving Willoughby with two of the vessels but no navigator to guide them. Not that it would have mattered much. At the Kola Peninsula, the pack ice forced both of his ships to over-winter.

Not one man lived to tell the story, but Willoughby's diary indicates that they struggled on, at least until Christmas. Legend has it—wrongly, of course—that a Russian fishing party found Willoughby in his cabin with pen in hand and the rest of the crew frozen in their tracks, performing their duties. The third ship, however, survived the storm, and under the command of Richard Chancellor, the crew reached Moscow from the White Sea. In their footsteps followed an overland fur trade with Russia that was to last for several centuries.

In 1556, another Muscovy ship under the command of Stephen Borough managed to get far enough northeast to sight the Kara Sea. Evidently news of his and Chancellor's forays spread through Europe, for the Dutch, who were already whaling and cod-fishing in northern waters and establishing themselves as a center of European commerce and agriculture, began tracking subsequent British exploratory ships to the Kola Peninsula. The aim evidently was to establish trade with Russia. One of the driving forces behind this Dutch interest was Oliver Brunel, an indefatigable entrepreneur who eventually reached Moscow and gained the trust of the Russians. In fact, it was the Russians who suggested that he undertake a northeast journey to China on their behalf. Brunel, however, chose to go home to sell the idea to his fellow entrepreneurs.

Not much is known about the Northeast Passage expedition which Brunel and other Dutchmen financed in 1584. Although it resulted in nothing of consequence, it helped set the stage for the most famous of Dutch Arctic expeditions in the 1590s. The third and last of these voyages involved Willem Barents and was remarkable not only for its discoveries—the islands of Spitsbergen (part of Svalbard) and Novaya Zemlya were mapped—but also for the fact that it was the first European expedition to experience and survive an Arctic winter. The decision to over-winter, however, was by no means intentional. After reaching Spitsbergen on June 19, Barents and Jan Corneliszoon Rijp had decided to separate eleven days later; Rijp retreated to Bear Island, while Barents pressed forward to Novaya Zemlya. On rounding the northern tip of that treeless island, Barents found his way blocked by ice and, before he could retreat, was enclosed by the moving floes, the power of which was so great that it "seemed the ship would be overthrowne in the place."

With no other option but to face the "great cold, poverty, misery and griefe" of the oncoming winter, Barents and his men resigned themselves to

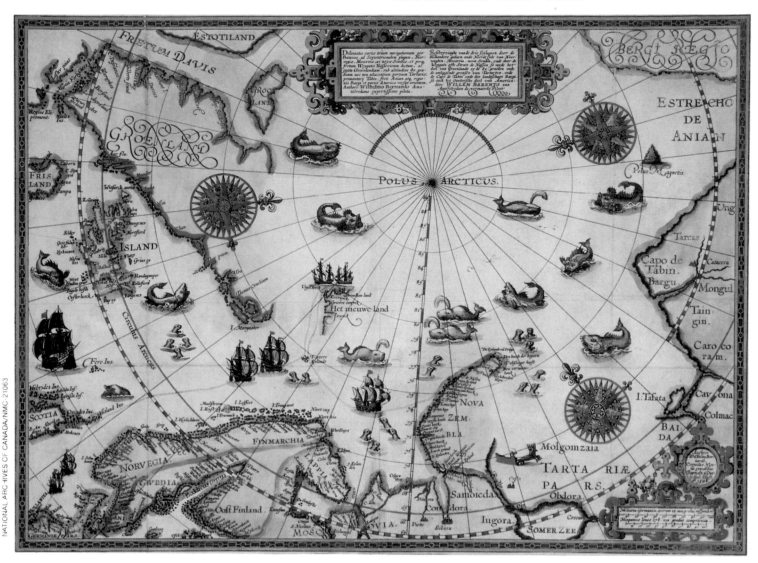

*Apart from the Vikings, Willem Barents and his crew were the first Europeans to successfully over-winter in the Arctic. This 1598 map shows his explorations.*

building a driftwood shelter and toughing it out until the following spring. Over the next several months, the crew spent a good part of their time in darkness, climbing outside through the chimney because the door was blocked by huge snowdrifts, and fending off curious polar bears—one had killed two of their crew the previous summer. Crippled with scurvy, the men kept themselves alive by eating Arctic foxes.

The long dark nights and the frequent blizzards so imprisoned Barents and his crew that, for days at a time, they didn't dare stick their heads out the chimney of their hut. Even a great fire, hot enough to burn their skin on one side, could not keep their backs and feet from freezing. Still, the Dutch sailors endured the winter with remarkable willpower. They amused themselves playing a game resembling golf on the sea ice, bathing in a makeshift steam house, and listening to the foxes scurrying on the roof of their shelter. No doubt, they felt that God was on their side as well, for when the sun rose for the first time that winter, on January 24, twelve days earlier than expected, they attributed it to his "almighte power."

When spring finally arrived in early June, the men were so weak, they nearly gave up all hope of returning home, especially when they found they were unable to drag one of the small boats from the shore to the hut for repairs. They had planned to use open boats as a means of escape if it became evident that the crushed ship would not be released by the ice or could not easily be

35

*The death of Willem Barents was depicted in an 1837 children's book, among other places, such was the extent to which exploration captured the popular imagination.*

repaired. Barents, however, refused to concede defeat and urged his healthier shipmates on. According to Gerrit de Veer, his display of willpower and courage bolstered the spirits of the crew, and the necessary strength was mustered to haul in and repair the boats.

The Dutchman's troubles were far from over. With the receding ice came more polar bears, some of which played a ghostly game of hide-and-seek as they moved in and out of the fog. On clearer days, as many as thirty could be seen at a time. At least twice, bears were within a few footsteps of catching one of the fleeing sailors. The sailors managed to kill some, yet even this proved to be unfortunate, for the men's bodies rejected the vitamin-rich liver of the animals with nearly fatal results.

By mid-June, the boat repairs were completed. With starvation a certainty if they waited any longer they set out for home in the open boats. Three months later, after battling gale-force winds from the northwest and averting starvation by stealing birds' eggs from the sides of cliffs, the beleaguered crew arrived on the Kola Peninsula. A Dutch ship was waiting, but Barents was not one of the celebrants. He had died from the effects of scurvy.

Not all was lost in these unsuccessful attempts to find a northeast passage. After the turn of the century, the Dutch focussed their attention on whaling in the Arctic seas between Greenland and Novaya Zemlya and wrested control of the Russian trade away from the English.

It was England under Elizabeth I that dominated the early search for a northwest passage. Thanks in part to Francis Drake's successful voyage around the world, the new queen lent her enthusiastic support to the building of a powerful maritime force. It was, however, Sir Humphrey Gilbert who provided the intellectual stimulus. In *A Discourse of a Discoverie for a New Passage to Cathia* (1576), after consulting the best geographers, maps, and charts of the time, he came to the conclusion that a northwest route "through a sea which lieth on the Northside of Labrador, mencioned and prooved, by no smal number of the most expert, and best learned amongst them," was the only practical route. No matter that part of his thesis was inspired by rumors that Martin Chaque, a Portuguese sailor, had passed, in 1555, through the Strait of Anian, taking him from the Pacific to the Atlantic in latitude 59 degrees near Newfoundland. The Northwest Passage was there, and was England's to find if the desire was there as well.

Gilbert was not alone in his enthusiasm for finding the Northwest Passage. Richard Hakluyt, for example, was writing *The Principal Navigations*, a compilation of navigational fact and economic information, as a deliberate attempt to promote national confidence during this era. In effect, the process of exploration was undergoing a dramatic transformation in England, just as Thorne earlier had hoped it would do.

It was, however, an ambitious merchant by the name of Michael Lok who pounced on the idea and secured from the Queen a charter for the establishment of the Company of Cathay. This was a significant breakthrough in the search for the Northwest Passage given the Muscovy Company's monopoly on exploration rights and its emphasis on a passage by way of the northeast. Sensing that the extraordinary opportunity called for extraordinary decisions, the Company of Cathay directors chose Martin Frobisher to lead its first expedition. A Yorkshire native who had once defied the Portuguese monopoly by participating in the African trade, he had also been called in by the Privy Council to answer to charges of piracy. Frobisher was not known to be a skilled navigator, so Lok no doubt had come to the conclusion that the job called for someone brash and daring, not an individual who played by the rules.

Frobisher did not fail them. A little more than a month after he and thirty-five men set out in 1576 in two barks, the *Gabriel* and the *Michael*, a severe storm cast the *Gabriel* on its side, and the ship quickly filled with water. All but Frobisher were certain that the *Gabriel* would sink. "The captyne," says one of the surviving manuscripts describing the voyage, "with valiant courage, stood up, and passed alongst the ship's side, in the chayn wales [channels], lyin on her flat syde, and caught holde on the weather leche of the foresaile; but in the weather-coyling [going about] of the ship, the fore-yarde brake. To ease her, the mizen mast was cut away...and as soon as practicable, the poor storm-buffeted bark was 'put before sea'; and all hands were set to work to prepare for the damages." A few weeks later, the crew sighted the shores of Newfoundland, sailed northward and entered a "a great gut, bay, or passage, divided as it were, by two main landes or continents, asunder." Frobisher was convinced that he had found the Northwest Passage to the Orient.

For this reason, Frobisher has been called the first pioneer of northern exploration. There is no question that many others preceded him. He himself saw the stone houses of whalers on his "Meta Incognita" (the coast of Frobisher Bay on Baffin Island), and there is no question that the Greenlanders had landed on the shores of both Newfoundland and Baffin Island beforehand. Frobisher's expeditions stand out, however, because they seemingly confirmed the existence of a passage. They also provide us with the first detailed description of the new lands and of the aboriginal people who became so important to future Northwest Passage searches.

More than 200 years later, the great nineteenth century whaler/scientist William Scoresby Jr. was to remark that "what we wish to be true, we readily believe; a maxim which, however doubtful in general, fully applied to the

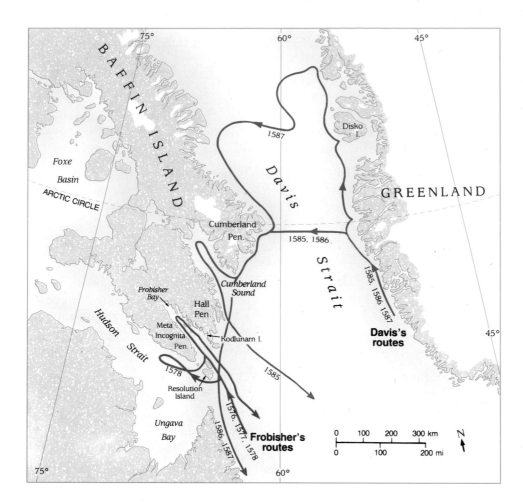

The Voyages of Martin
Frobisher (1576, 1577, 1578)
and John Davis
(1585, 1586, 1587)

northern voyages of discovery." If he had any particular voyage in mind, it must have been Frobisher's. After returning to England empty-handed, his career as an explorer should have been over. But among the souvenirs brought home by his crew was a rock "much like sea cole in colour" that found its way into the hands of the wife of one of the adventurers. By chance, she threw the rock into a fire, and upon retrieving it, doused it for some reason with vinegar, "where-upon it glistened with a bright marquesset of golde." Lok's own version claims that the sample was actually given directly to him. Both versions of the tale end with everyone certain that gold had been discovered.

Not surprisingly, funding for a second voyage was immediately forthcoming. Although disguised as "one intended to God's Glory, the benefit of al Christendom, and the honour and profit of this realm," the real aim was clearly designed to please the creditors. So was the goal behind the third voyage. This time the backers stepped forward so quickly with their money that they were blind to the fact that the 200 tons of rock that had been brought back by Frobisher on the second journey was worthless pyroxenite and amphibolite. Marked by protracted skirmishes with the Inuit and a failed attempt to establish a mining colony on Baffin Island, these last two forays represented the worst of England's new-found aspirations. In one of the battles, at least six Inuit were killed and several taken hostage. One old native woman, suspected by the crew to be either a devil or witch, had her footwear torn off to determine if she had cloven feet. In another battle, Frobisher was struck in the backside by an arrow. The behavior of the Englishmen towards one another was no better. Apparently exasperated by the loss of one of the fifteen ships on the third voyage, Frobisher reputedly had half a dozen men flung overboard when the rudder of another ship was broken. Their efforts to repair it left them "half-dead" by the time the job was done and they were lifted back into the boat.

Lok was thrown in prison for exploiting the greed of the others and bankrupting the Company of Cathay after the true nature of the ore was firmly established. Frobisher, however, escaped punishment—he really had nothing to do with the fraudulent representations that were made about the value of the ore his ships brought home. Although he was anything but popular with the government and investors, he redeemed himself as a senior officer in the war with Spain in 1588 and as one of Drake's accomplices in the piratical assault on the West Indies. Before he died in 1594 in a skirmish with the Spaniards, he was rewarded with a knighthood.

It is difficult to imagine a more striking contrast to Frobisher's voyages than the first of three that John Davis led eight years later. Davis was a remarkable individual, as considerate towards his men as they were devoted to him, and particularly gracious to the Greenland Inuit. The first encounter was an enchanting one. Davis had just landed on shore to search for wood and water when he found a small shoe and pieces of sinew strewn about the shoreline. "Then we went upon another Island on the other side of our ships," recalls the voyage's chronicler John Janes, "and the Captaine, the Master, and I, being got up to the top of an high rocke, the people of the country having espied us, made a lamentable noyse, as we thought, with great outcryes and skreetchings: we hearing them, thought it had bene the howling of wolves." Davis was determined to show the Inuit no harm. The chamber quartet was called down from the ship to strike up some music and the crew began to dance. It wasn't long before ten kayaks pulled up to shore. Their paddlers climbed out and greeted the Englishmen with friendly embraces.

The gesture of goodwill was evidently appreciated. Early the next day, thirty-seven Inuit kayakers reciprocated with a rousing drum dance for the sleeping shipmates. "Whereupon we manned our boats and came to them..." wrote Janes, "and after we had sworne by the sunne after their fashion, they did trust us. So I shook hands with one of them, and he kissed my hand, and we were very familier with them. We were in so great credit with them upon this single acquaintance, that we could have anything they had."

Davis seemed to be destined from childhood to conduct this voyage. Born in Sandridge where there was a "most delightsome prospect to behold the barks and boats to pass and repass upon the river," his neighbors were the Gilberts, whose second son was none other than Humphrey. As a scholar and sailor, Davis was also well-versed with the latest discourses on the subject of the Northwest Passage, including those of Richard Hakluyt.

The encounter with the Inuit was typical of the kind of good fortune and good sense that Davis and his crew experienced and followed for the remaining part of the journey. The ships sailed northwards along the Greenland coast to Mount Raleigh in waters "altogether voyd of ye pester yce" and then crossed the strait that now bears Davis's name, to Baffin Island near Cumberland Sound. They had no idea that this was the spot that Frobisher had discovered nearly a decade earlier. On shore, there were signs of people everywhere: a sled; a carved wooden image; a bird made of bone; the skull of a human; and twenty dogs, which they thought were wolves until they noticed one was wearing a collar. There was no living person to be seen.

*Sir Martin Frobisher had the heart and soul of a pirate. He was just the kind of man English merchants wanted to lead a search for the Northwest Passage.*

Davis continued to sail up the sound, but was eventually forced by strong winds to make a retreat to England. There, he confidently reported that "the northwest passage is a matter nothyne doubtful at anye tyme almost to be passed, the sea navigable, voyd of yce, the ayre tolerable, and the waters very depe."

The second journey was to prove otherwise. The plan this time was to send one ship up the east coast of Greenland in search of a polar route, while Davis retraced his first journey westward to the southwest tip of Greenland. Davis encountered the same group of Inuit and was given a rousing welcome. However, the situation soon deteriorated. The Inuit—reportedly—couldn't resist stealing cables, clothes, and other metal objects aboard the ship. Davis was at first tolerant of their thievery, but when they made off with the ship's anchor, he had evidently had enough. Stones were hurled in both directions before the altercation was abruptly ended with gunfire. In an effort to recover the anchor, Davis kidnapped one of the Inuit, hoping to use him as a hostage. The plan, however, failed when the Inuk died.

The situation did not improve. Sailing northwards along the old route, Davis was stopped by a massive ice floe, the likes of which he had never seen or expected, given the ice-free conditions of the previous year. Over the following two weeks, the cold, damp weather seriously affected the health of his men, forcing him, midway through the journey, to send one ship home with the sickest members. He continued southwest, but missed Cumberland Sound and Frobisher Bay in stormy weather before anchoring off the coast of Newfoundland, loading up with some fish, and sailing home.

On his return, Davis mysteriously declared: "I have now full experience of much of the Northwest part of the world, and have brought the passage to that certainty, as that I am sure it must be in one of foure place." Perhaps he concluded that the worst was behind him. The investors, however, were leery about sending yet another uninsured expedition off with nothing to show in return for the previous one. They finally agreed on the condition that Davis devote two ships to fishing and the third to discovery.

Beset by ship problems almost from the beginning, Davis again followed the Greenland coastline, this time making it as far as Sanderson's Hope on the west Greenland coast before heading westward to Baffin Island. The voyage's only significance is that he almost certainly discovered Lancaster Sound, the entrance to the true Northwest Passage, before heading south once more along the east coast of Baffin Island and to England.

Although Davis failed three times to find the Northwest Passage, there is probably no other Arctic explorer of his era who made a more significant contribution to Europe's understanding of the New World and the people who inhabited it. His descriptions of native culture, influenced by his fascination with the occult ("they are witches and have many kinds of inchantments, which they often use, but to small purpose, thanks be to God"), are the first recorded ethnographic study of the Inuit. And like the best Northwest Passage explorers to follow—Leopold McClintock and John Rae to name but two—he was innovative, always searching for ways to improve his chances for discovery. His back staff, for example was a marked improvement on instruments for measuring the height of the sun, while his *Traverse Book* became the model for ships' logs. Most important of all was his contribution to the first English terrestrial globe created by Emery Molyneaux (1592). Davis was able to pin-

*Sphagnum moss and Arctic cottongrass. Explorer Robert Hood noted in his detailed journal of the first Franklin expedition that Cree women lined their cradleboards with this moss.*

point with some accuracy the entrance to Hudson Strait, which became the focus of the search for the Northwest Passage in the seventeenth century. Ironically, had Davis been given one more chance, he would almost certainly not have chosen that route to follow. The most practicable passage, he correctly believed, lay somewhere off the strait that now bears his name.

Davis never did get another chance to test his theory. Investors simply weren't interested in devoting more funds to a cause that had provided them with no return in the past. And then there was Britain's battle with the Spanish Armada. Davis was determined to do his part. By the time it was over, he took what he could get—a South Seas trade mission in which he discovered the Falklands. His life came to an end in 1605 at the hands of pirates in the East Indian seas he had so desperately tried to reach by a northwesterly direction.

Only Robert Bylot and William Baffin managed to sail farther north than Davis over the course of the next two centuries—a testament to Davis's navigational skills and good fortune. Yet, again, there is an ironic twist to this famous voyage in 1616. Bylot and Baffin had sailed their *Discovery* up Greenland's west coast, past Davis's farthestmost point at Sanderson's Hope, and "into an open sea, in the latitude of 75 degrees 40 minutes, which anew revived our hope of passage." This was the North Water, the recurring polynya that was to intrigue explorers for the next 250 years and lend greater credence to the notion of an open polar sea. The North Water eventually led the *Discovery* to Lancaster Sound where Baffin morosely observed that "here our hopes of passage began to lesse every day then other, for this sound to the southward we had a ledge of ice betweene the shoare and us, but cleare to the seawarde." Little did he know how close Bylot and he were to finding what they and so many others had been searching for.

If one man's name has become synonymous with Europe's search for the Northwest Passage in the seventeenth century, it is that of English explorer Henry Hudson. His first attempt in 1607 to reach the Orient, however, was not through the strait that today bears his name, but in the direction of the North Pole, a route that Thorne had advocated nearly a century earlier. It was a hopeless undertaking, given the faith that Hudson had put in the existence of Zeno's Engroeneland. The second attempt a year later by way of the northeast, in the path of Barents, was no more successful. Nevertheless, it had its moments, albeit some strange ones. The entry Hudson made in his log on June 14, 1608, tells the story:

> *This morning, one of our companie looking overboord saw a mermaid, and calling up some of the companie to see her, one more came up, and by the time shee was come close to the ship's side, looking earnestly on the men: a little after, a sea came and overturned her: from the navill upward, her backe and breasts were like a woman's, as they say that saw her, her body as big as one of us; her skin very white: and long haire hanging downe behind, of colour blacke, in her going downe, they saw her tayle, which was like the tayle of a porposse, and speckled like a macrell.*

Since the Muscovy Company was not interested in financing more mermaid sightings, Hudson was forced to go out of the country for further support.

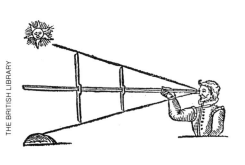

*John Davis, shown using a cross-staff, was arguably the most talented and insightful of the early English explorers who set out in search of the Northwest Passage.*

The Dutch East India Company willingly obliged, hoping that he might, this time, find success in the direction that Barents had tried and failed. Hudson was introduced to Barents's former adviser, the geographer Peter Plancius, before the voyage. Somehow, Plancius had obtained the journals of English explorer George Weymouth, whose voyage to the northwest in 1602 held out some hope that the waters that would later be known as Hudson's Strait might prove to be the passage. While Plancius apparently dismissed the possibility, it must have made an impression on Hudson. In 1609, he was commissioned by the Dutch East India Company to find a northeast passage around Novaya Zemlya. Faced later on with the threat of mutiny from a Dutch crew that wanted no part of the polar challenge, Hudson rerouted to more temperate climes. Believing, as some did at the time, that a passage was located in the latitude of 40 degrees, he eventually reached the present-day site of New York City and sailed up the river which now bears his name. His report later paved the way for the settlement of what was then known as New Amsterdam.

Hudson returned soon after, determined to continue on with the northwest search the following year. The Dutch would have renewed their contract with him had it not been for the English government's accusing Hudson of acting against the well-being of his country. In the end, it mattered little to Hudson, as a syndicate of merchants stepped forward to finance his fourth voyage. Within two months of sailing from England, he had passed through the strait that now bears his name and into the "spacious sea" he was certain would lead him to the East Indies. Heading in a southerly direction, he was stopped by land at the edge of James Bay—too late in the season to make a safe retreat back home.

What ensued stands as one of the grimmest episodes in the search for the Northwest Passage—a fitting parallel to the experiences of Willoughby and Barents. Hudson's ship had been stocked with only a six-month supply of food, and his men were unsuitably outfitted for the cutting winds that make the southern Hudson Bay region as cold as places hundreds of miles farther north. Hudson himself simply did not have the leadership skills of a Barents to rally the crew. If anything, he made an already explosive situation worse by court-martialing one man, demoting another, and replacing both with individuals who had demonstrated no talent or loyalty in the past. One of the men replaced was Robert Bylot, the ship's navigator and leader of future Northwest Passage expeditions.

Any vestige of goodwill or camaraderie that survived the winter vanished the day the ship was freed from the ice in mid-June. Expecting to sail home immediately, the crew was bluntly informed by their captain that the search for the passage would continue. A number of the crew, including the men that Hudson had promoted, revolted. Hudson, his son John, and seven men, five of whom were ill, were taken prisoner and shoved into a boat with only a musket and a kettle. According to one crew member, the aim was simply to convince Hudson to return to England and increase the food rations. But when Hudson managed to pull the small boat up to the ship by its tow rope, the true intent of the mutineers became apparent. One cut the rope while the others stood by silently. The outcasts disappeared into the expanse of the open bay and were never seen again.

Only nine men survived the treacherous voyage back to England. One starved to death; two were disemboweled by hostile Inuit during a landing on

*Henry Hudson on his third voyage in 1609, painted by George Wharton Edwards.*

## The Search Through Hudson Bay

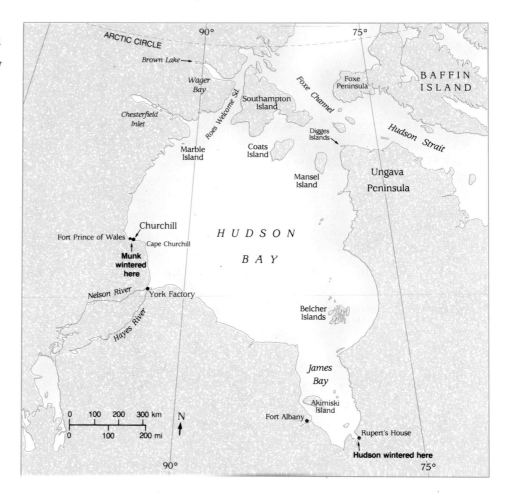

Digges Islands at the northwest end of Ungava Peninsula; and the remainder were in such a weakened state that only Bylot was left standing when they sighted the coast of Ireland. Bylot escaped trial, perhaps because of the excitement aroused by his assertions of discovery, and he was dispatched the following year to search for both Hudson and the Northwest Passage. Four of the other seven men who were brought to trial were acquitted, even though a previous inquiry had ruled that there was enough evidence to justify their hanging.

If a pattern of exploration emerged in the early maritime search for the Northwest Passage, it was in the uncanny tendency for successive voyages to repeat the horrible experiences of their predecessors. That thought must have crossed Danish sea-captain Jens Munk's mind in 1620 when he found himself marooned near present-day Churchill, Manitoba, only a few hundred miles from Hudson's icy refuge. Cognizant of the frigid winter ahead of him, Munk tried desperately to find ways of averting the effects of scurvy. He ordered his men to eat roots and berries until the supply disappeared with the season. Then, one by one, the men died and had to be hauled to a nearby hilltop to be buried. It wasn't long before the survivors didn't have the strength to do even that. When spring arrived, only three of the sixteen crew members were still alive. And poor Munk was confronted with the almost impossible task of navigating his vessel home.

The return voyage to Norway took sixty-seven days through stormy seas. As ignominious as it was to return a failure, Munk suffered a further indignity after one of his men stabbed another in a tavern brawl. As their captain, Munk

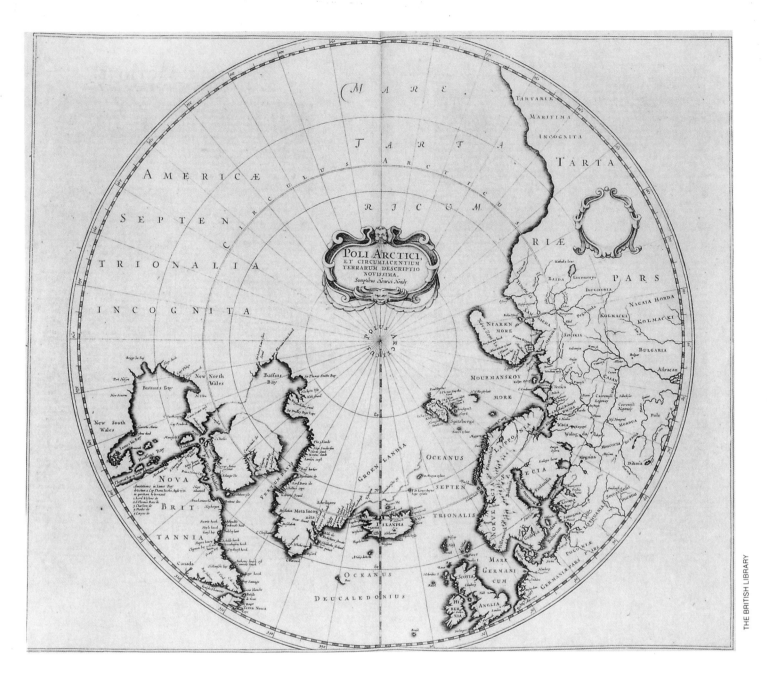

was held responsible for their conduct and was arrested. To make matters worse, no one was particularly eager to see him released. It was three months before the king of Denmark made the necessary arrangements. And even then, he ordered the sick and travel-worn captain to turn around immediately for another attempt to discover the Northwest Passage. Surprisingly, Munk was willing; however, word about his terrible experiences had spread throughout Denmark and Norway so rapidly that he was unable to find enough volunteers to make another try.

For those who dared search its waters, Hudson Bay continued to be pitiless. In 1612–13, Thomas Button, with Bylot aboard, spent yet another grim winter at the mouth of the Nelson River between present-day Churchill and York Factory. Two years later, William Gibbons was blocked by ice before he could even enter the bay, and Thomas James (1631–32), in what has to be one of the most peculiar mishaps, very nearly perished in a forest fire that he accidentally started. Perverse as it might seem, the British seemed to thrive on

*A map of the Arctic published in the English-language edition of the 1636 Mercator-Hondius atlas, following the voyages of Luke Foxe and Thomas James.*

these sorts of perilous adventures. Those like Luke Foxe, whose competent exploration of Hudson Bay showed that "further search...this way is hopeless," and who returned to England with everyone in reasonable health, were snubbed, seemingly for not having endured a winter.

It was Hudson himself who best summed up the futility of a northwest passage through the bay that bears his name. "If the passage be found," he told Bylot in 1610, "I confess there is something gained in the distance, but nothing in the navigation. For allow that this passage falls into the South sea; if it does, little good is like to ensue of it because of the hazard of cold, of ice, and of unknown seas which experience must teach us."

The search for the Northwest Passage through Hudson Bay continued for the next 200 years. From the time of Hudson to the day the British Admiralty entered the search in 1818, at least thirty-six ships were sent out to find the passage—thirty-three commanded by the British. James Hall, Benjamin Jones, William Hawkridge, Thomas James, James Napper, Robert Crow, Christopher Middleton, William Moor, Francis Smith, Charles Swaine, Constantine Phipps, Richard Pickerskill, James Cook and Walter Young—all were added to the list of captains who had tried and failed. From 1500 on, only once was the search abandoned for more than twenty-five years and only four times was there ever a gap of fifteen years between voyages. Yet, none was to find the narrow passage to the northwest waters that lay in Fury and Hecla Strait, a most unpromising channel that separates Melville Peninsula from Baffin Island and joins the Gulf of Boothia and Foxe Basin.

*An exhausted, dehydrated young arctic fox, encountered by the photographer after a severe wind storm.*

*Yearling caribou on Southampton Island, which was first explored by Christopher Middleton on his 1741–42 voyage.*

# ARCTIC WILDLIFE

*A hardy Arctic hare on Ellesmere Island.*

The red of dwarf birch and the yellow of
dwarf willow blend on an Arctic slope.

The first frost of autumn forms on the crimson
leaves of bearberry. European traders and
explorers learned from the Cree Indians to
mix tobacco with the dried leaves of this
plant to give it a milder flavor.

49

A young ringed seal. These small seals are
the main prey of polar bears.

A rough-legged hawk chick.

*Two male polar bears wrestle on the shores of*
*Hudson Bay.*

"Nowhere did I see anything worthy of your pencil. So much for the country. It is a barren subject, and deserves to be thus briefly dismissed."
—EXPLORER JOHN RICHARDSON IN A NOTE TO GEORGE BACK WHILE TRAVELING OVERLAND ON THE ARCTIC COAST IN 1821.

# 3.

# ACROSS THE
# BARREN LANDS OF
# NORTH AMERICA

T he geographer J. Wreford Watson once stated that the popular image of an unknown land is compounded of what men hope to find, what they look to find, how they set about finding it, and how those findings fit into their existing framework of thought. When you travel the rugged 93-mile (150-km) shoreline of Wager Bay, from Hudson Bay to Brown Lake, the meaning of Watson's statement becomes all the more clear. Wager Bay is a long inlet stretching into the tundra of the Keewatin region. The mouth of the bay is deceptively narrow, and it is easy at first to mistake it for a river. But then it widens quickly, producing tidal pressures at its mouth and head. These tidal pressures are so powerful that they cause waterfalls to reverse and patches of water to remain ice-free in the coldest days of winter.

For the neophyte Arctic traveler, Wager Bay's rocky bluffs, gently rolling lowlands, and grey skies reinforce the pre-existing notion of the "Barren Lands"—a term used by non-natives to describe the surrounding countryside. But to an Inuit hunter, a land and seascape such as this one is far from barren. The tundra is, at various times of the year, teeming with caribou, and the open water of the bay is a magnet for whales and seals in need of breathing holes in winter, for polar bears who prey on them, and for migratory birds searching for food and resting spots in early spring.

To an eighteenth-century European explorer searching for the Northwest Passage, however, Wager Bay represented something entirely different. For Christopher Middleton, in 1742, it initially offered hope of locating the

*Limestone spires tower over the Northwest Passage on Baffin Island's Brodeur Peninsula.*

53

Northwest Passage to the Orient. But when the former Hudson's Bay Company man, who had made "three and twenty" voyages to Hudson Bay previously with the company, sent a small boat off to explore further, he discovered that the tide came south from Roe's Welcome Sound. It was a strong indication that no passage led through it. And so the man who had traveled farther northwest than any other European had prior to that time, returned to England that summer convinced that further search for the passage in Hudson Bay was futile.

Nothing seemed to have gone well on Middleton's voyage, despite his competence as a navigator. He had sailed the previous autumn as far as Coats Island but was forced by the advance of cold weather to over-winter near the newly constructed Prince of Wales fort at Churchill. James Isham, the governor, was an old acquaintance, but he would have preferred that Middleton's crew, whom the commander himself described as "a set of rogues, most of whom deserved hanging," had gone elsewhere. Middleton didn't improve the situation either. His prodigious distribution of alcohol both for pleasure and medicinal purposes likely exacerbated relations with the Hudson's Bay Company men as well as the scurvy that broke out among the crew. Of the thirteen who died that winter, eleven succumbed to the ravages of that terrible disease. But Middleton's most serious misfortune arose out of the fact that the reality of his first-hand discovery at Wager Bay did not fit into the fantasy of Arthur Dobbs, the man who had been responsible for his appointment to the Royal Navy in the first place and for his subsequent commission to search for the Northwest Passage. In the end, the fiery, highly influential landowner rejected Middleton's conclusion about the prospects of passage through Wager Bay. In a public fit of temper, he accused the veteran Hudson's Bay Company man of accepting a £5000 bribe from his former employers "to return to their service, and not to go the Voyage [in search of the Northwest Passage], or to go in pursuit of it to Davis's Streight, or any other Way that he was ordered upon."

An official inquiry had no alternative but to clear Middleton of the allegation, since the facts rested heavily in his favor. But such was the popular image of Hudson Bay, and the hopes of a passage extending from it, that Dobbs was still able to gather enough public support to sponsor a second attempt. In the process of complaining so loudly about Middleton and the Hudson's Bay Company, he persuaded Britain's parliamentarians to offer a reward of some £20,000 to any person other than a naval officer who discovered the passage.

Dobbs's obsession with the idea of a northwest passage through Wager Bay was colored in part by his jealousy of the Hudson's Bay Company and the monopoly on trade it enjoyed in the New World. An ardent free-trader and ambitious entrepreneur, he charged that its directors had "slept on the shores" of that icy body of water in contempt of its charter obligation to search for a passage to the East. While it is obvious in hindsight that Dobbs's accusations arose out of his own desire to exploit the New World's resources, his attacks on the Company nevertheless stirred it into action, and together with the Royal Navy and the rival North West Company, the Hudson's Bay Company eventually became an important player in an overland search for a northwest route to the East.

Despite Dobbs's ranting, there was a rationale for the Hudson's Bay Company's reluctance to search for the Northwest Passage. Most important was the fact that nowhere in the charter granted to the directors in May 1670 is it stipulated that searching for the Northwest Passage is mandatory. Second previous efforts by the Company to do so had met with failure.

The most notable of these early searches by the Hudson's Bay Company —that of James Knight between 1719 and 1722—was conspicuous because it ended so tragically. Knight's story began in June 1719 when the Company approved his plan to "find the Strait of Anian" that Martin Chauque and others were purported to have found over a century earlier. In this case, the directors were also interested in "gold and other valuable commodities" that they thought might be found. Two ships, *Albany* and *Discovery*, were outfitted and Knight sailed with Captain David Vaughan into Hudson Bay. When winter set in, they anchored in a harbor at Marble Island, 7 miles (11 km) off the mainland coast, ostensibly because Knight feared an attack by the Inuit. It was a fatal mistake. Both ships were apparently damaged while trying to enter the harbor at low tide. All fifty men were forced to find food and shelter on a wind-scarred rock outcrop that was only 10 miles (16 km) long, 3 miles (5 km) wide, and no more than 300 feet (92 m) above sea level.

Many years later, Inuit told Samuel Hearne of the Hudson's Bay Company that sickness and famine had killed all but twenty of Knight's men by the second winter. The following spring, there were only five remaining, and they, according to Hearne's report,

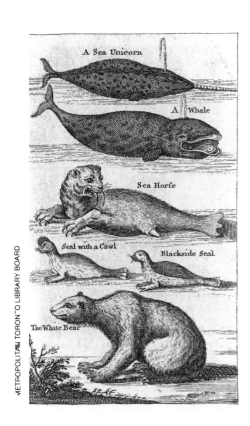

*were in such distress for provisions that they eagerly (ate) the seal's flesh and whale's blubber as they purchased it from the natives. This disordered them so much that three of them died in a few days, and the other two, though very weak, made a shift to bury them. Those two survived many days after the rest, and frequently went to the top of an adjacent rock and earnestly looked to the South and East, as if in expectation of some vessels coming to their relief. After continuing there a considerable time toget'.er, and nothing appearing in sight, they sat down close together and wept bitterly. At length one of the two died, and the other's strength was so far exhausted that he fell down and died also in attempting to dig a grave for his companion.*

Geographer William Barr attributes the tragic fate of the expedition in part to the friction between Knight and Henry Kelsey, the governor of the Hudson's Bay Company at Fort Prince of Wales. Kelsey did little to provide Knight with advice or instructions on his voyage and specifically ordered him to stay away from the Company's posts unless there was an emergency. When Knight failed to return the following year, Kelsey did nothing about it. Some people back in England optimistically assumed that the passage had been found, and that Knight had gone through it into the South Sea. But Kelsey must have known better, given the failures of so many previous voyages in Hudson Bay and the long-standing doubts at Fort Prince of Wales that a passage through it even existed. Yet no attempt was made until 1721 to search for the missing men. Not until forty-eight years later was the true fate of the expedition uncovered, when Hearne learned of it from Inuit in the area.

Whether appointing Hearne to search for an overland route to the Orient in 1768 constituted atonement for past wrongs, such as that done to James Knight, is difficult to say. Hearne, however, lent some credibility to the

The illustration on the left side shows:
A Sea Unicorn
A Whale
Sea Horse
Seal with a Cawl
Blackside Seal
The White Bear

*Arctic animals drawn by Henry Ellis on William Moor's 1746 voyage to discover the Northwest Passage.*

possibility in 1795 when he went to unusually great pains in his personal account of his travels to defend the Company against criticism. "The air of mystery, and affectation of secrecy, perhaps, which formerly attended some of the Company's proceedings in the Bay might give rise to those conjectures," he conceded. But those writers "advance such notorious absurdities, that none except those who are already prejudiced against the Company can give them credit." Doubtless, Hearne would not have been so enthusiastic in coming to the Company's defence had more been known about the details surrounding Knight's unfortunate plight. Then again, perhaps the Hudson's Bay Company may not have reacted as diligently in the face of Dobbs's criticisms had it not felt a little guilty about its lackadaisical search for the passage in the years before dispatching Hearne.

Hearne's show of loyalty was an admirable one, given the nightmares he himself was forced to endure at the hands of Moses Norton, his superior in the Company at Fort Prince of Wales. Twice, in 1769 and 1770, in pursuit of an overland passage and the copper that was fabled to lie at the mouth of the Coppermine River, Norton provided him with an Indian guide, "the first capable of committing any crime, however diabolical," the second a man of no standing among his fellow Indians. As a result, Hearne twice returned in failure. It was only with good luck and circumstances that he finally crossed paths with the Chipewyan Indian Matonabbee, who successfully guided Hearne across the Barren Lands in 1770–72 on an epic overland journey from Fort Prince of Wales to the mouth of the Coppermine River. With that journey, Hearne almost certainly became the first European to see the Arctic Ocean.

Hearne's accomplishment ranks high with several other early pursuits of overland passage to the Pacific Ocean, including that of James Stewart in 1715–16, when he traveled some 680 miles (1100 km) by land from York Factory to an area south of Great Slave Lake, and Alexander Mackenzie's sighting of the Beaufort Sea in 1789, and of the Pacific Ocean in 1793. In 1819–22 and 1825–27, British naval officer John Franklin led two overland expeditions in which 1000 miles (1600 km) of new territory was mapped out, including all of the unexplored Arctic coastline, save a 150-mile (242-km) section between Icy Cape and Point Turnagain in the west and the area that lies between Point Turnagain and Repulse Bay in the east.

It would be wrong to denigrate the importance of these journeys. Given the territory that was covered and the physical toll from cold, hunger, mosquitoes and blackflies, they are worthy of mention. They also contributed significantly to European understanding of the unknown lands. But, as Canadian historian Michael Bliss remarked on the 200th anniversary of Mackenzie's journey down the river that still bears his name, "What kind of 'discovery' is it when Englishmen or Scotsmen are guided through country known to and inhabited by North American natives [when] most of the 'exploration' of what is now Canada consisted of...natives show[ing] whites the routes they normally took through their territory?"

Hearne's three overland journeys tell the story. Far from being a master of his own fate, he was little more than a slave to the whims and aspirations of all three of his principal Indian guides. Chawchinahaw, the first of them, apparently had no intention of taking Hearne to the Coppermine. Instead, he robbed and then deserted him about 200 miles (320 km) outside of Fort Prince of Wales on the Barren Lands, forcing Hearne and his European

HUDSON'S BAY COMPANY ARCHIVES/PROVINCIAL ARCHIVES OF MANITOBA

*Hudson's Bay Company trader/explorer Samuel Hearne made three overland journeys in search of the Northwest Passage. This portrait was painted in 1787 after his return to England.*

companions to abandon the trek and drag their gear back on their own. Conne-e-quese, the second guide, was little better. Although "a steady man and an excellent hunter," he apparently had no idea where he was going, and having no standing among the Indians of the area, did nothing to stop them from behaving as if Hearne "had brought the Company's warehouse" along or stealing what he would not give up.

Matonabbee was an altogether different figure. The son of a slave woman who had been traded to the Hudson's Bay Company, he had been orphaned at an early age and raised by Richard Norton, the father of Hearne's nemesis at Fort Prince of Wales. At six feet, he was unusually tall for that time, but it was his mastery of Chipewyan, Cree and English, combined with his own keen intellect, that made him a peacemaker among rival aboriginal groups in the region, and consequently a man of considerable importance to the Hudson's Bay Company. Even with Hearne, who considered Indians to "differ so much from the rest of mankind, that harsh uncourteous usage seems to agree better with the generality of them...than mild treatment," Matonabbee commanded complete respect. "In conversation, he was easy, lively and agreeable, but exceedingly modest; and at the table, the nobleness and elegance of his manners might have been admired by the first personages in the world; for to the vivacity of a Frenchman, and the sincerity of an Englishman, he added the gravity and nobleness of a Turk; all so happily blended, as to render his company and conversation universally pleasing."

Reading Hearne's narrative, one suspects that a friendship blossomed between the two. During their eighteen months together, they talked of religion ("he [Matonabbee] had so much natural good sense and liberality of sentiment...as not to think that he had the right to ridicule any particular sect"), of Indian sorcery ("of which he was a perfect bigot"), and of Matonabbee's fondness for Spanish wines ("he never drank to excess"). Yet, Hearne was as much a hostage to Matonabbee as he was to the other guides. When, for example, Matonabbee and his Indian companions embarked upon the slaughter of a group of Inuit camped at a waterfall near the mouth of the Coppermine River, Hearne could do nothing but stand by and watch the horrible event unfold. "The shrieks and groans of the poor expiring wretches were truly dreadful," he recalled years later, "and my horror was much increased at seeing a young girl, seemingly about eighteen years of age, killed so near me, that when the first spear struck into her side she fell down at my feet, and twisted around my legs, so that it was with difficulty that I could disengage myself from her dying gasps." Hearne pleaded for her life, but to no avail. Her killers simply ignored him and drove their spears into her body. "Then they looked at me sternly in the face, and began to ridicule me, by asking if I wanted an Esquimaux's wife," said Hearne.

Hearne's helplessness, however, was as much a consequence of his own ineptitude as it was of the superior talents of his aboriginal guides. Even when it came to the simple job of preparing meals, he seemed unable to cope. Indian custom, for example, dictated that the murderers at Bloody Fall had to abstain from cooking either for themselves or for others until they were rejoined with their people and had performed specific rituals that would effectively wash the blood from their hands. Had all of the Indians participated in the slaughter, the job of cooking would have fallen to Hearne, a prospect he himself viewed as being "no less fatiguing and troublesome than humiliating and vexatious."

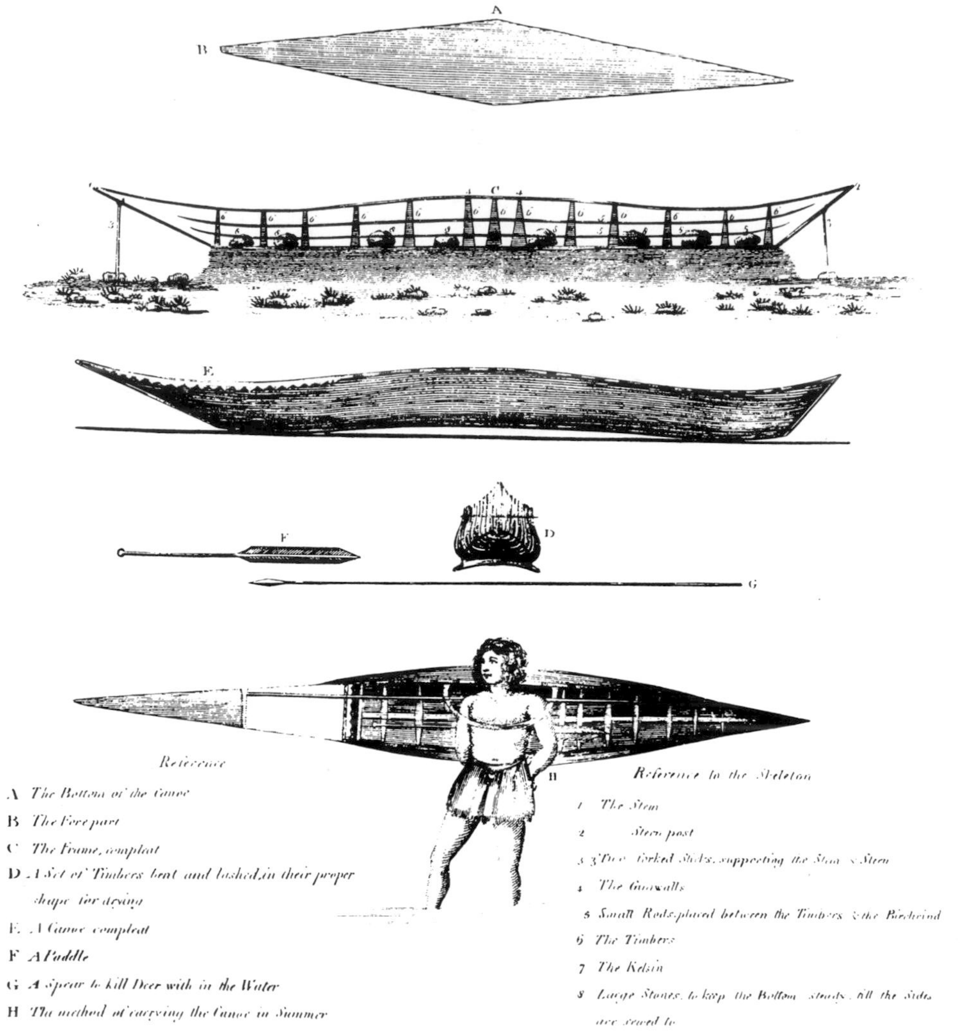

Samuel Hearne's drawing of the construction of an Indian canoe.

*Reference*

A  The Bottom of the Canoe

B  The Fore part

C  The Frame, compleat

D  A Set of Timbers bent and lashed in their proper shape for drying

E  A Canoe compleat

F  A Paddle

G  A Spear to kill Deer with in the Water

H  The method of carrying the Canoe in Summer

*Reference to the Skeleton*

1  The Stem

2  Stem post

3  3 Two forked Sticks, supporting the Stem & Stern

4  The Gunwalls

5  Small Rods placed between the Timbers & the Birchrind

6  The Timbers

7  The Kelsin

8  Large Stones, to keep the Bottom steady, till the Sides are sewed to

Fortunately for Hearne's vanity and self-esteem, it turned out that two of the Indians had not participated in the bloodshed, and they were able to perform the chores.

One can't help but admire Hearne's courage and tenacity, whatever his personal weaknesses might have been. At one point, he walked for three long days "and not tasted a morsel of anything except a pipe of tobacco and a drink of snow water." On another occasion, Hearne's feet were so badly injured in walking the rocky terrain that his toenails "festered and dropped off" and every subsequent step he took "left the print of my feet in blood." Yet, for all that Hearne learned and endured during the eighteen-month journey with Matonabbee, he returned home empty-handed. No mine was established, and no passage was found.

Nothing so daunting as a massacre or an eighteen-month trek loomed over Alexander Mackenzie in 1789 while he canoed down the river the Dene (Indians of the Mackenzie Valley) call Deh Cho, or on his overland trek to the Pacific in 1793. But, in his bid to expand the North West Company's trade with discovery of a northwesterly route to the Orient, the Scottish fur trader did borrow a chapter from Martin Frobisher's book of strategy, using threats and violence to force native hunters to guide him along the way.

Although only seventeen years separate the last of Hearne's journeys and the first of Mackenzie's in 1789, the image of the unknown land, what the

Europeans were looking for, and why and how they set about finding it had changed dramatically. No longer was Hudson Bay the focus of the search for a passage to the East. Instead, all eyes now were on an overland route to the northwest Pacific, in response, in part, to Spain's claim to Nootka Sound in 1774, Russian trading expansion into Alaska, and Captain James Cook's attempt in 1776–78 to find Bartholamew de Fonte's apocryphal northwest passage to Baffin Island. (In 1708, a London magazine published a fictional account of a letter purported to have been written by a man named de Fonte, who suggested that he had discovered a northwest passage from the northwest Pacific to Baffin Island in 1640. Although the letter was likely composed by the magazine's editor, it nevertheless excited considerable interest. Several expeditions, including George Vancouver's exploration of the west coast of Canada and Alaska between 1791 and 1795, were sent out in search of the Passage. It was Vancouver who finally proved that it did not exist.) Mackenzie's mentor, Peter Pond, believed that Cook's Inlet near Prince William Sound might, in fact, be the mouth of a river that flowed from Great Slave Lake. For Mackenzie and the North West Company, confirming this theory would have been extremely important, since it would have given the Company the opportunity to register a counterclaim to Spain's sovereignty initiatives on the northwest coast and prevented the Russians from making any further incursions into the North American interior.

It is difficult to imagine Mackenzie's voyage down the Deh Cho as being as arduous as Hearne's or Stewart's overland treks, in spite of the fact that he managed the 3100-mile (5000-km) return trip in just 102 days. In 1789, the paddle from Fort Chipewyan on Lake Athabasca to the Beaufort Sea was as much a summertime float down a well-used transportation corridor as it is today. Aside from the rapids of the Slave River and the relatively minor ramparts of the Mackenzie, the only serious hazards were paddling into the blustery headwinds and navigating through the delta at the mouth of the river. Seldom were there days when Mackenzie did not encounter Indian or Inuit camps along the way, and he relied on the aboriginals almost exclusively for food and for provisions, and even for paddling his canoe. And, as he was frequently to do on his voyage to the Pacific in 1793, he used whatever means necessary, even kidnapping, to compel reluctant aboriginals (he called them "conductors") to guide him.

Unlike Hearne, Mackenzie did not seem to grow with his experiences. From the beginning to the end of his days in the northwest, his vision of the unknown land and the people who inhabited it was as pessimistic as it was unsympathetic. "I think it unpardonable in any man to remain in this country who can afford to leave it," he told a friend shortly after reaching the Pacific. He believed the Indians' stamina, their intelligence, even their appetite were inferior to his own, despite the fact that he had depended upon them as much as Hearne had. When one aboriginal party abandoned him in the night, for example, he sent his European comrades chasing after them. "I could not do well without them," he confessed.

For all that he accomplished, Mackenzie dismissed the importance of sighting the Arctic and Pacific oceans. In a letter to Lord Dorchester, the Governor of British North America, he lamented that his Arctic expedition "did not answer the intended purpose." It merely proved that Pond's "assertion was nothing but conjecture, and that a Northwest Passage is impractical."

59

The overland route to the Pacific, he later concluded, was too arduous, thus making a viable trade link between the Atlantic and Pacific untenable. So, seemingly with no regrets, Mackenzie put an end to his exploring days before the arrival of his thirtieth birthday. He married into wealth, obtained a significant share in a reorganized North West Company, and then embraced the opportunity to leave.

By 1815, one would have expected that the prospects of a commercially viable passage through the northwest of Canada would have all but faded with the journeys of Hearne and Mackenzie, and with the subsequent demise of the North West Company's trade in the Mackenzie district, resulting from financial mismanagement. Yet, the most serious search for the Northwest Passage was really just about to begin, partly because the end of the Napoleonic Wars had left the British government with the dilemma of finding something to do with a navy it had worked so hard to build up, but also because of the new view of the Pacific northwest that resulted from James Cook's remarkable voyages between 1776 and 1778.

Cook revolutionized the process of discovery that Thorne had tried and failed to change in his time. According to Stephen J. Pyne, Cook's voyages were special because they combined new skills of navigation with new purposes of discovery. Ultimately, Cook's systematic mapping of the North Pacific, together with Hearne's and Mackenzie's exploration of the northwest interior, eradicated the necessity for cartographers to hypothesize as Mercator did about the shape of the New World and the prospects of a route through it. The unknown land now had real dimensions and carefully mapped-out coastlines. In essence, the Northwest Passage was no longer merely a product of the imagination.

No individual articulated the possibilities that arose out of this new Age of Enlightenment, at least as they pertained to the discovery of the Northwest Passage, better than John Barrow Jr. Playing on the hopes and aspirations of the nation, he engineered a national plan for discovery that would have pleased the likes of Robert Thorne and Richard Hakluyt. Ironically, Barrow was by birth of farming stock. But perseverance, energy, ambition, and circumstances earned him the title of Second Secretary to the Admiralty, the powerful job of administering the internal affairs of the Royal Navy. Barrow's goal of putting the navy to good use in peacetime following the Napoleonic War may just as easily have focused on the further exploration of Africa where England's interests also lay. But it was an earlier voyage to Greenland on a whaling ship that convinced him that nothing was "more honorable and useful" than to complete the scientific and hydrographical work that men such as Cook and George Vancouver had initiated.

Barrow's plan was a three-pronged one—a search for the Northwest Passage via Baffin Bay; another by way of the mythical open polar sea; and a third by overland trek in the footsteps of Stewart, Hearne, Mackenzie, and the aboriginals who guided them. Barrow's choice of leader for the overland expedition was John Franklin, a pudgy, gentle soul from a prosperous family of merchants. One of twelve children, he first went to sea on a merchant vessel at the age of thirteen. But family connections eventually got him a position in the Royal Navy. His credentials for the job of leading an overland search for the Northwest Passage, however, consisted of little more than having completed a coastal survey of Australian waters, having fought in a battle against Napoleon's fleet in 1805 in which the blast of guns permanently damaged his

*Alexander Mackenzie once said that the "practicability of penetrating across the continent" was "the favorite project of my own ambition." Although he succeeded, he returned to Scotland with no desire to return to North America.*

hearing, and having made a near-disastrous attempt under David Buchan's command in 1818 to find Barrow's open polar sea via the east coast of Greenland. Such was Franklin's vision of the unknown land and how to go about finding a passage across it, however, that George Simpson, the Hudson's Bay Company's governor, confidently predicted that he would fail miserably. Not only were Franklin and his men ill-equipped and inexperienced, according to Simpson, but Franklin himself lacked "the physical powers required for the labor of moderate Voyaging in this country; he must have three meals p diem, Tea is indispensable, and with the utmost exertion, he cannot walk Eight miles in one day, so that it does not follow if those Gentlemen are unsuccessful that the difficulties are insurmountable."

In many respects, Franklin's appointment reflected just how much imagination continued to play a role in finding a passage through the unknown land in spite of cartographers' ability to draw a more realistic picture of where it might lie. Franklin's orders, as fantastical as they were, tell the story. With surgeon-naturalist John Richardson, midshipmen George Back and Robert Hood, Scottish seaman John Hepburn, and four Orkneymen, he was instructed to proceed from the shores of Hudson Bay to Cumberland House, then north to Great Slave Lake via Fort Chipewyan and on to the mouth of the Coppermine River. From there, they were to explore the uncharted Arctic shoreline towards Hudson Bay and meet up with Sir William Edward Parry, the naval officer who had been dispatched in the same year by Barrow to find the Northwest Passage via Lancaster Sound by ship. Along the way, Franklin and his men were to study the land, the natives, the natural history, and the aurora borealis—a tall order for a group of sailors, whichever way one looked at it.

Franklin and his party must have looked quite a sight when they set off from York Factory on September 9, 1819. Included in the load they brought with them from England were magnets, three sextants, two azimuth compasses, several artificial horizons, twelve thermometers, a theodolite, a barometer, a dipping needle, a transit instrument, and an electrometer. Each officer carried a compass, a spyglass and a chronometer. They also brought along blank leather-bound notebooks, large sheets of paper to protract each day's journey, manuals on navigation and astronomy, books of exploration by Hearne and Mackenzie, and at least three natural history textbooks. There were bibles, prayer books, scripture commentaries, and at least one surgical text that Richardson carried. They had brought so much food from England that they had to leave stores of bacon, flour, rice and tobacco at York Factory; another 1200 pounds (545 kg) of sugar, biscuits, tea, rice, and portable soups eight days later at Rock House on the Hayes River; and 640 pounds (290 kg) of moldy pemmican at Methy Portage the following July. Yet they ended up being short of guns, knives, ammunition, meat, and other goods throughout the course of their travels. As a result, a number of them had to make several long and arduous trips back to North West Company and Hudson's Bay Company posts to augment their supplies. On one return trip, Back snowshoed a total of 1200 miles (1932 km). None of these supply missions, however, was entirely successful. With the Hudson's Bay Company and the North West Company at war with each other, there was a shortage of the goods they required.

As it turned out, Simpson was not far off the mark in his assessment of Franklin and his men. Throughout the journey, they behaved as if they had never left a naval ship. They were fond of wearing their decorations and

*A portrait of John Franklin.*

Resting Place on a Winter's Night *was sketched by Robert Hood on Franklin's first overland expedition, 1819–22. The camp was along the Clearwater River south of Lake Athabasca.*

uniforms and hoisting the Union Jack whenever they found occasion to do so. Upon meeting Matonabbee's stepson, for example, they presented him with a medal as if he were a loyal British subject. Franklin himself described the situation best while comparing the four Orkneymen who eventually abandoned him at Fort Chipewyan, to British seamen:

> *I was very much amused with the extreme caution these men used before they would sign [on]; they minutely scanned all our intentions, weighed every circumstance, looked narrowly into the plan of our route, and still more circumspectly to the prospect of return. Such caution on the part of the northern mariners forms a singular contrast with the ready and thoughtless manner in which English seamen enter upon any enterprise, however hazardous, without inquiring, or desiring to know, where he is going, or what he is going about.*

For all the attention paid to manners and deportment, these naval officers could not help but be drawn hopelessly into the primitiveness of their situation on occasion. The combination of prim and primitive instincts produced some rather bizarre behavior. The effeminate Robert Hood and the "overbearing" George Back, for example, developed such a rivalry over a fifteen-year-old Copper Indian girl named Green Stockings that they fought a duel for her affections. (Green Stockings later bore a child who was listed in the census as "orphaned daughter of Robert Hood, R.N.") Fortunately for both men, Hepburn had unloaded the charges from their pistols beforehand. Then Franklin, seeing a need for emotions to cool down, sent Back off on his formidable snowshoe trek to pick up more supplies.

That Franklin and his men got as far as they did can be attributed in part to the crew of voyageurs who were hired on at Cumberland House. These French

Canadian adventurers were traditionally used by the Montréal fur merchants to trade and set up alliances with the Indians. There were also the interpreters Pierre St. Germain and Jean Baptiste Adam; and Ferdinand Wentzel, the North West Company clerk at Fort Providence. But it was Wentzel's hiring of the Copper Indian Chief Akaitcho (Big Foot) that prevented the expedition from ending in complete disaster. Big Foot and the 200 Copper Indians who comprised his group of Chipewyans had for many years supplied the North West Company with meat. But their true claim to fame was the ferocious manner in which they pillaged furs and stole women from their Dogrib and Hare Indian neighbors, who occupied the area to the west and northwest of Great Slave Lake.

Like Matonabbee, Akaitcho was an intelligent, independent individual who set his own rules, regardless of what Franklin had in mind. Although he initially agreed to guide Franklin's party down the Coppermine River to the Arctic Ocean in one season, he backed out in August 1820, citing as reasons the "slow mode of travelling" of the Europeans and the imminent "advance of winter." At the same time, Akaitcho proved to be very empathetic in difficult situations. When Franklin stubbornly insisted that he would push ahead to the Arctic coast on his own, Akaitcho reluctantly acquiesed.

After conferring with his officers that night, Franklin announced to Akaitcho the next morning that he was relinquishing his plan. Rather than trek to the coast, he would build a fort (Enterprise) at Winter Lake and wait until the following summer.

All went relatively smoothly that autumn and winter. In September, Franklin, Richardson, and Hepburn hiked overland on a scouting journey with an old Indian named Keskarrah to the Coppermine River, leaving Wentzel in charge at Winter Lake to oversee the construction of the buildings. On his return from Fort Providence, Back brought along two Inuit interpreters named Junius and Augustus. They had come all the way from Churchill to Fort Resolution on the south shore of Great Slave Lake. Newspaper reports

*Robert Hood's drawing of Green Stockings, a Copper Indian who later bore his child.*

NATIONAL ARCHIVES OF CANADA/C-5528

*This cliff was named Rocky Defile by John Franklin on his overland trip to the Copper-mine River.*

delivered to Franklin announced that King George III had died, but Franklin concealed it from the Indians, "lest the death of their great Father might lead them to suppose that we should be unable to fulfill our promises to them." What he couldn't conceal, however, was the disdain the traders frequently vented at them behind their backs. The man in charge of the Fort Providence post, for example, had apparently told Akaitcho that, far from being what the explorers represented themselves as, Franklin and his men "were merely a set of dependent wretches, whose only aim was to obtain subsistence for a season in the plentiful country of the Copper Indians" and that "out of charity," they had been supplied with goods by the trading companies, "but that there was not the smallest hope" of them being able to pay Akaitcho and his men. With this news, Akaitcho might have been wise to carry on with his own business and not bother to return to Fort Enterprise the following spring. But he was, according to Franklin, a man of his word and, despite the vindictive rumors, was there with him at Winter Lake when he and his party of twenty set off for the Coppermine the following June.

True to the tradition established by Hearne and Mackenzie, the aboriginals did all the hunting on the trip, while the voyageurs were left to take care of the more onerous tasks of paddling the boats, cooking the meals, and carrying whatever needed to be transported overland. The weight was considerable, at times overwhelming. The British officers never once thought of lending a hand, even when it might have speeded progress at critical times.

The fate that awaited Franklin and his men, however, was influenced by much more than the naval officers' unwillingness to participate in mundane tasks. From the outset, all attempts by Augustus and Junius to establish relations with the Inuit of the area failed, leaving Franklin with no clue about the countryside he was heading towards, nor any opportunity to purchase food. Even worse, Akaitcho remained true to his word and returned south once the expedition reached the mouth of the Coppermine River. With his best hunters gone halfway through the trip, Franklin found himself with little more than three days' supply of pemmican by the time the party reached Point Turnagain on the Kent Peninsula, still well over 500 miles (800 km) from their intended destination at Hudson Bay. There were no caribou in sight, and no hint of Inuit encampment anywhere. The necessity of "putting a speedy termination to our advance" was clear, but for some reason, Franklin decided to push on for another five days. They were five days he could ill afford.

By the time the decision was made to return on August 18, the season had changed with a vengeance. Snow remained on the ground, small pools were covered with ice, and the party was down to its last half-bag of pemmican. In addition, blustery winds and stormy seas made boating back along the Arctic coastline to the Coppermine River all the more hazardous and exhausting. Finally, the decision was made to head south into Bathurst Inlet rather than continue along the coast. The idea was to travel in as straight a line as possible back to Fort Enterprise. According to Richardson, only "the privation of food under which our voyageurs were at present laboring, absorbed each other's terror, otherwise the most powerful eloquence would not have induced them to attempt such a traverse."

Once at the mouth of Bathurst Inlet, Franklin and his men set off for Fort Enterprise. They found the long hike across the tundra a torturous one. By the time they reached the banks of the Coppermine River, the voyageurs were in

open revolt, having been reduced to eating putrid caribou meat and boiling the leather from their clothing and old shoes. Junius had disappeared, Franklin was fainting from exhaustion, and Hood was suffering from acute diarrhea. Worst of all, the party had arrived without the canoes that were necessary to ferry across the river. Apparently they had been jettisoned by the voyageurs to lighten the load. Franklin was furious. Initial attempts to raft across the river failed. Then, Richardson nearly drowned in the icy waters, trying to swim across with a line of rope. Finally, after a week, a boat was made out of canvas and bedding. Once across the river, the expedition divided into three parties. Back was sent ahead with three voyageurs in the hope that he would find Akaitcho and bring him back with supplies. Franklin carried on with the largest group, towards Fort Enterprise. Richardson and Hepburn remained behind with Hood, who was deathly ill and unable to travel.

Few events in the long history of the Northwest Passage are as mysterious or controversial as that which unfolded in the days following the departure of Back and Franklin's two groups. The Iroquois voyageur Michel Teroahauté had gone along with Franklin, but returned very soon afterwards to Richardson's camp. There, he produced a note from Franklin stating that both he and Jean Baptiste Bélanger were unable to continue on, that they were to return to Richardson, and that a mile ahead lay a stand of pine trees that would provide a better shelter for them all. Teroahauté explained to Richardson that he and Bélanger had earlier parted ways, as Bélanger was eager to proceed ahead of him. Teroahauté assumed that he had gone astray as he himself had found the route back difficult.

Neither Richardson nor Hepburn had any reason to doubt the story. But then a series of strange events occurred—telling incidents that Richardson was able to piece together only with time. First, Teroahauté led Richardson and Hepburn to the stand of pines with such confidence of its location that it belied his description of the route as difficult. Then Teroahauté disappeared with an axe, leaving Richardson and Hepburn to return alone to the tent where Hood had remained. The following evening, he reappeared with some

*George Back's journey down the Great Fish River (renamed the Back River on his return to England) is depicted in his drawing* Interview with the Esquimaux of the Thleweechodezeth.

strange-tasting meat that he said had come from a wolf that had been gored by a caribou buck. "We implicitly believed this story then," Richardson wrote in his journal, "but afterwards became convinced from circumstances, the details of which may be spared, that it must have been a portion of the body of Bélanger or Perrault." (Ignace Perrault was one of the voyageurs who had followed Bélanger and Teroahauté back unbeknownst to Hepburn or Richardson.)

Had Teroahauté killed Bélanger and Perrault or did he butcher them after they had died from exposure? Richardson and Franklin later traded notes and deduced that Bélanger had been murdered first. When Perrault caught up, Teroahauté had killed him as well, if only to cover up his crime. Of course, neither Richardson nor Hepburn had any suspicions at the time. But as Teroahauté's behavior and comments became more and more sinister and erratic over the course of the next few days, they eventually put two and two together. "Michel refused to hunt, or even to assist us in carrying a log of wood to the fire, which was too heavy for Hepburn's strength and mine," Richardson wrote. "Mr. Hood endeavored to point out to him the necessity and duty of exertion, and the cruelty of [his recently announced decision to head south on his own] without leaving something for our support; but the discourse far from producing any beneficial effect, seemed only to excite his anger, and amongst other expressions, he made use of the following remarkable one: 'It is no use hunting, there are no animals, you had better kill and eat me.'"

The morning Teroahauté was scheduled to depart on his own, he showed no sign of moving. Instead, he lingered about the fire "under the pretence of cleaning his gun," according to Richardson. There was little choice but to carry on with the normal tasks; morning service was read, and then, at around noon, Richardson and Hepburn removed themselves a short distance from camp to gather wood for a fire and lichen from the rocks. Hepburn was close enough to hear an argument break out between Hood and Teroahauté back at the camp, but apparently thought nothing of it. Then a shot was fired. Richardson assumed at first that one of the two men was cleaning his rifle. But then Hepburn called out and both of them returned to find Hood lying dead with a bullet in his forehead. Richardson initially thought that "in a fit of despondency, [Hood] had hurried himself into the presence of his Almighty Judge, by and act of his own hand." But Teroahauté's strange behavior, and his insistence that he had nothing to do with it, caused Richardson to consider otherwise. Upon closer inspection of the body, he "discovered that the shot had entered the back part of the head, and passed out at the forehead, and that the muzzle of the gun had been applied so close as to set fire to the night-cap behind. The gun, which was of the longest kind supplied to the Indians, could not have been placed in a position to inflict such wound, except by a second person."

Now, more than ever, Richardson and Hepburn believed their lives were in danger. Certain they could not survive an open attack, given Teroahauté's superior strength—he had two pistols, an Indian bayonet, and a knife in his possession—they conspired to kill him at the first opportunity. Hepburn offered to take on the task, but Richardson declined. "I determined, however, as I was thoroughly convinced of the necessity of such a dreadful act, to take the whole responsibility upon myself; and immediately upon Michel's coming up [from a rock where he was supposed to be gathering the lichen], I put an end to his life by shooting him through the head with a pistol." It was not a

*In* Expedition Landing in a Storm, 1821, *drawn by George Back on Franklin's first overland expedition, the British officers watch as the voyageurs unload the boats.*

moment too soon, according to Richardson. There was no evidence that Teroahauté had stopped to gather any lichen at all. Instead, it appeared that he had been loading his gun so that he could kill them both.

Over the course of the five days that it took to get back to Fort Enterprise, Richardson's journal makes no further mention of the murder. Perhaps staying alive was all that mattered, for he does say that they could "scarcely drag our limbs after us." Any expectation of a warm welcome at Fort Enterprise, however, was quickly dashed when they were finally reunited with their comrades. "No language that I can use being [is] adequate to convey the wretchedness of the abode, in which we found our commanding officer," Richardson wrote that day in October. "The greatest part of the house had been pulled down for firewood, and that the only entire chamber which was left, was open to all the rigor of the season, the windows being but partially closed by a few loose boards." But it was the "hollow and sepulchral sound" of the inhabitants' voices and their emaciated appearance that had drove home the horror of the situation. A winter was still ahead of them, and there appeared to be no relief in sight.

Only nine of the twenty original members survived Franklin's overland expedition across the Arctic tundra. Because four of them were officers, and only two voyageurs, there was a great deal of subsequent speculation that they had knowingly participated in cannibalism, an allegation that has never been substantiated. Certainly all of them would have perished had it not been for Akaitcho and his men responding quickly to Back's plea for help when he finally arrived at the camp from the Arctic coast. Akaitcho's rescue party made the 55-mile (86-km) trip to Fort Enterprise in just two and a half days. Richardson later said that the Indians "wept on beholding the deplorable condition to which we were reduced." Then they "cooked for us and fed us as if we had been children, evincing a degree of humanity that would have done honor to the most civilized nation."

Nothing, however, more accurately reflected Akaitcho's true character than what occurred when the survivors were strong enough to make the journey back south to his camp and then onto Fort Providence. There, Akaitcho learned what the traders had warned him about—that the payment for his services had not arrived. To this he replied philosophically, "The world goes badly; all are poor, you are poor, the traders appear to be poor, I and my party are poor likewise; and since the goods have not come in, we cannot have them. I do not regret having supplied you with provisions, for a Copper Indian can never permit white men to suffer from want of food on his lands, without flying to their aid." Expressing his trust that the payment would eventually be made, Akaitcho added, with a sense of humor, "it is the first time that the white people have been indebted to the Copper Indians."

When Franklin and his party returned to England in 1822, it was to a hero's welcome normally reserved for those who had fought courageously in war. Their reception might have been different if the public had been aware of the alleged cannibalism or of the murder of Teroahauté. As it turned out, Richardson did provide a confidential report to the Admiralty, outlining what had taken place during that "dreadful" moment on the tundra, but the original has never been found. In any event, the Admiralty evidently never acted upon it, whatever it might have contained. However, Ferdinand Wentzel, the North West Company clerk, went to his grave believing that the British

*Franklin's guide, Copper Indian Chief Akaitcho, and his son.*

Attack of the Polar Bear *appears in an anonymous officer's account of his adventures on Parry's first voyage in 1819.*

officers had been guilty of "unpardonable want of conduct" and that Richardson deserved to be punished for the murder of Teroahauté. To this day, historians are still debating the issue. The circumstances, however, as reported by Franklin and Richardson, favor the case for self-defence.

Franklin's was not the only navy-backed expedition that might have blurred Barrow's vision of the unknown land or dampened his hopes of finding a passage through it. By 1824, Sir William Edward Parry had already failed in two attempts to find a passage by sea, once by way of Lancaster Sound (1819–20), the other through Hudson and Repulse bays (1821–23). In 1824, George Francis Lyon was unsuccessful in his attempt via Hudson Bay to reach Point Turnagain, the most easterly point reached by Franklin. Nevertheless, Barrow, it turned out, was more determined than ever to continue the pursuit, for another war of sorts had broken out. Only this time it wasn't the French threatening stability in Europe, it was the Russians taking a stab at the pride and potential commerce associated with British exploration in the North Pacific. In 1821, the Russians decreed that no foreigners were to venture into the Bering Sea or to Pacific-coast regions of Russian America. Apparently, they had designs of their own on that part of the world, having dispatched Kotzebue in 1816, and Vasily'ev in 1820 and 1821, on voyages of discovery.

Barrow's response to the Russian activity in the Pacific northwest would have been understandable if the plan he eventually embarked upon hadn't been so remarkably similar to the one he had chosen in 1819. This time Parry would once again try to find the Northwest Passage by way of Lancaster Sound, and on through either Prince Regent Inlet or Barrow Strait. Franklin and Richardson would travel overland to the Arctic sea along Mackenzie's route down the Deh Cho. Once at the mouth of the great river, they would split up. Richardson was to travel eastward along the coast to meet up with Parry. Franklin was to head west in order to rendezvous with Captain William Frederick Beechey. Beechey had been assigned to take the ship *Blossom* from the Pacific to Bering Strait, then eastward along the uncharted coastline.

Only three years had elapsed since Franklin's return to England, but the European presence in the wilds of North America had changed dramatically in that short time, even if the strategies of the Royal Navy in exploring it hadn't. The North West Company and the Hudson's Bay Company amalgamated in March 1821, renewing the emphasis on opening up the unexplored interior. None of this would have much mattered to Franklin had the amalgamation not corresponded with a shift in aboriginal control away from Akaitcho and his Yellowknives to the Dogribs, whom they had treated badly for so many years. With the apparent approval of the new company, the Dogribs conspired to destroy Akaitcho's power by ambushing and killing thirty-four of his people at a camp located between Great Bear Lake and Great Slave Lake. The traders eventually interceded to end the feud, but Akaitcho vowed never to travel through that country again. "Our hearts will be with [you]," he told Franklin by way of messenger when the British explorer arrived once again at the area of Great Slave Lake in 1825, "but we will not go to those parts where the bones of our murdered brethren lie, for fear our bad passions should be aroused at the sight of their graves, and that we should attempt to renew the war by recollection of the manner of their death."

Fortunately, Franklin had learned some lessons from his previous nightmare-crossing of the tundra. The boats he used this time were of sturdy mahogany rather than fragile birchbark, and he made some concessions to

*A drifting iceberg strikes one of William Edward Parry's ships on the night of June 29, 1821, in this sketch by Peter Rindisbacher.*

waterproof clothing, even if animal skins would have made better outerwear. But his faith in British know-how was as strong as ever as he saw it prudent to replace the troublesome voyageurs with British seamen.

Nonetheless, all went relatively smoothly during that summer of 1825. By mid-August, Franklin and his group had retraced Mackenzie's voyage down the Deh Cho and arrived on the delta in time to view the fabulous spectacle of an ice-free Arctic sea with whales and seals "frolicking in the waves." It was a bittersweet moment for Franklin as he planted the silk flag that his recently deceased wife, Eleanor, had given him. Like any stalwart British officer, Franklin did his best to conceal his grief from the men, not wanting the occasion to undermine the joy they were sharing at having come so far, so quickly. There was no thought, however, of pushing on, as Franklin had hoped to do the first time he saw the Arctic sea. Instead, he returned to a site on Great Bear Lake that had once been used as a trading post by the North West Company, but now was reopened by the Hudson's Bay Company. No longer so scornful of Franklin, Governor Simpson had pledged his undying support for the expedition, quite evidently because he, too, was concerned about Russian incursions into the northwest interior.

After spending the winter at Great Bear Lake in June 1826, the expedition party set off once again. From the Mackenzie delta, Franklin and George Back headed west with their old friend Augustus while Richardson and his party went east with another Inuk, named Ouligbuck, who had been hired in the Churchill area by the Hudson's Bay Company to assist the expedition. Right from the start, it was a different kind of journey. The Inuit who were so scarce on the first expedition were encountered almost immediately on the second. However, the first encounter with a group of about 200 did not go as Franklin had expected or wished. When Augustus informed them that the Europeans had come to the region to open up trade with them, pandemonium ensued. The Inuit made off with everything they could lay their hands on, including the buttons on the officers' naval jackets. Only Franklin's cool head and his orders not to shoot averted what would almost certainly have been a massive slaughter. The Inuit returned the following day and apologized for

*Esquimaux Coming Towards the Boats was drawn by George Back on Franklin's second overland expedition.*

*George Back's watercolor* Autumnal View of Fort Franklin and Part of Bear Lake Taken from the Northward.

their behavior. The prospects of obtaining such valuable items, they said, had simply overwhelmed them.

Fortunately, Franklin maintained this cool demeanor throughout the course of the journey along the Arctic coast. The party quickly reached the Clarence River, well within striking distance of the eastern boundary of Russian America. Franklin was sure he could reach Icy Cape and make the rendezvous with Beechey. But, as was the case on his first overland expedition along the Arctic coast, the weather was not at all accommodating. By mid-August, the group found themselves wandering aimlessly in an icy fog that cleared only when sleet and gale-force winds made any meaningful progress impossible. Confronted with the same decision he had faced at Point Turnagain five years earlier, Franklin was tempted to push ahead just as he decided to do before. Instead, he recognized that he had "higher duties to perform than the gratification of his own feelings." And so, without knowing that Beechey's land party was waiting for him just 160 miles (258 km) away, he retreated to Fort Franklin at Great Bear Lake.

Once again, Franklin was not the only one to return to England with bad news. Neither Beechey nor Parry had succeeded in their journeys either: Parry had to abandon one of his ships on the east coast of Somerset Island after ice drove it ashore and grounded it; Beechey returned from Icy Cape when Franklin and his men failed to show up. He spent the winter of 1826–27 in the Pacific, and then made one more trip back to the Bering Sea before returning to England. The Franklin expedition, however, was by no means a complete failure. Together, both Richardson and Franklin had mapped out a long new section of Arctic coastline without suffering the tremendous loss of lives that resulted from the first overland attempt. Franklin himself returned to England in 1827 convinced that completion of the passage was now within practical grasp. If only for "pride" and "enlightenment" rather than for any "immediate benefit to herself," he said, England should "not relax her efforts until the question of a northwest passage has been satisfactorily set at rest."

Given all that it had done to find the passage without success, the Admiralty would have rather put the whole matter of exploration in the Northwest to rest following Franklin's return to England. And it might have done just that had it not been for a chain of events sparked by the irrepressible

John Ross, who was still smarting from the humiliation he had suffered over the Croker Mountain affair. Ross was determined to try again to find the passage, and when Barrow and the Admiralty turned him down, he went to his friend Felix Booth, the fabulously wealthy gin merchant, for support. This he eventually got, but only after an ironic twist—the government canceled its £20,000 prize for the first man to find the passage in order to discourage Ross and others from making an attempt. As it turned out, it was just the thing Ross needed to get Booth's financial support, for the latter was unwilling to back an expedition until he could be sure that no one could interpret his involvement as a ploy for material gain.

At age fifty-two in 1829, Ross may have been past his prime, but he was miles ahead of the Admiralty in looking for ways to improve the prospects of finding the Northwest Passage. Lord Melville, for example, saw the introduction of steam to power maritime vessels as "calculated to strike a fatal blow to the naval supremacy of the Empire." Ross, however, welcomed it and published in 1828 *A Treatise on Navigation by Steam*. Steam-powered vessels, he reasoned, were particularly well suited to the Arctic because their power might ease the way through some forms of ice. They could also propel the ship on calm days and their shallow draft would allow closer approaches to unmapped coastlines.

Misfortune and circumstance, however, once again dogged Ross on his 1829 voyage. Part way through, he was forced to hoist the sails because the engines weren't working properly. But even then, he and his nephew James Clark Ross as second-in-command, were able to reach Parry's wreck on the gravel shores of Fury Beach on the east coast of Somerset Island by mid-August. From there they sailed another 300 miles (480 km) southward before the onslaught of winter forced them to consider retreating. By that time, however, it was already too late. The ice, said Ross, in describing what blocked his path homeward, is "stone.... These mountains of crystal hurled through a narrow strait by a rapid tide; meeting, as mountains meet, with a noise of thunder, breaking from each other's precipices huge fragments, or rendering each other asunder, till, losing their former equilibrium, they fall over headlong, lifting the sea around in breakers, and whirling it into eddies while the flatter fields of ice, formed against these masses." There was no choice for Ross and his crew but to find a place to spend the winter.

Four years went by, and not a word was heard from Ross. One might have suspected that Barrow and the Admiralty felt vindicated, since they had been opposed to both Ross and his modern ideas. But such was Ross's popularity among the general public that the government was forced to support a private expedition in 1833 to find him. The idea in this case was to find the source of the Thlew-ee-choh-desseth, or Great Fish River (now called the Back River), which was rumored to be located somewhere northeast of Great Slave Lake. The expedition would transport supplies along the river and then into Prince Regent Inlet, where Ross and his crew were believed to be. The man promoting this venture was none other than George Back, fresh from an extended holiday in Italy and eager to be back in the limelight.

All went relatively well during the first year of the expedition. Back wintered in a magnificent, multi-chimneyed log cabin built for him in the forest at the extreme east end of Great Slave Lake, adjacent to the Lockhart River. But well before his intended departure onto the Barren Lands, news

Snow Cottages of the Boothians *depicts Sir John Ross's party visiting an Inuit village on the Boothia Peninsula during Ross's second expedition, 1829–33.*

arrived that Ross and his crew were back in England. Ross had been forced to abandon his ship, *Victory*, near the south end of the Boothia Peninsula after two successive years of heavy ice failed to free her. All but one of the crew members survived the long ordeal back, thanks, in large part, to Inuit assistance and to supplies that Parry had left behind on Fury Beach. In the end, the party made it to Navy Board Inlet on Baffin Island just in time to rendezvous with the whaling ship *Isabella*, the ship Ross had commanded on his first Northwest Passage voyage in 1818.

Back was not upset by the news, for it freed him to concentrate his efforts on exploration and scientific studies. However, not everyone was as confident about the prospects that lay ahead as Back was. Hudson's Bay Company man William Mactavish sent a letter home to his family predicting that "you'll hear what a fine story they'll make out of this bungle, they will you may be sure take none of the blame themselves.... They will return next summer [1835] and like all the other Expeditions will do little and speak a great deal."

One suspects that it was the overbearing Back, and not simply the Hudson's Bay Company's traditional antipathy for naval explorers, that caused Mactavish to feel this way. Franklin himself had grave reservations about Back when he was planning his second overland journey. "You know, I could have no desire for his company," he told Richardson when Back offered his services, "but do not see how I can decline it if the Admiralty press the matter, without being of great disservice to him, and publicly making an exposure of his incapacity in many respects." And Thomas Simpson, the cousin of the Hudson's Bay Company governor, found Back "to be not only a vain, but a bad man."

Whatever his personal handicaps, Back had proved on both of Franklin's overland expeditions his ability for overland travel at which he was as skilled as any British naval explorer. And he would prove it once again, with the help of the Indian Maufelly (Augustus was supposed to be the guide, but he died en route to Great Slave Lake), by traveling down the Great Fish, one of the longest and perhaps the most formidable of the northern rivers. There are eighty-three major rapids or waterfalls in the 530-mile (853-km) stretch of water that snakes its way between Sussex Lake and Chantrey Inlet on the Arctic coast. Back and his party completed the journey in just thirty-one days.

Once on the Arctic coast, Back had hoped to make it to Point Turnagain, but ice stopped him at Point Ogle. From there, he could see King William's Land to the north, and to the northeast "a vast stretch of water and ice," beyond which he discerned there to be an open sea. This was in fact the Boothia Peninsula, and he wrongly suspected that a passage ran through it. However, it was August 15, and time was running out. So, the decision was made to retreat.

The Royal Society awarded Back its coveted Gold Medal when he finally returned to England in 1835, and the river was named in his honor. However, Back's trip down the Great Fish was not completed without controversy. Richard King, the surgeon-naturalist who had accompanied him, later returned to England—he had been left behind to wrap up loose ends and send supplies and equipment home. Boothia, he correctly surmised, was part of the mainland, and he charged that Back could have ascertained this himself if he had devoted more time and energy to confirming it. Instead, he sent three men with telescope and compass to find out: they returned with different stories about

*Although George Back was viewed unfavorably by Richard King, John Richardson and John Franklin, he was a talented artist and a competent outdoorsman.*

what they had seen (King later discovered that they had killed three Inuit in an altercation). Moreover, King believed that Back had beat too hasty a retreat, even though he had orders to return between August 12 and 20. A short while longer, he suggested, and they could have conducted the 116-mile (187-km) round trip to Boothia, thus confirming what he had all along suspected.

More than anything else, however, King was troubled by Back's recommendation against any further exploration down the Great Fish River, which he considered too shallow and hazardous. This was heresy, according to King, for it "it must be apparent to all persons that the Isthmus of Boothia cannot be approached more readily than by the [Great Fish River, as there,]...the difficulties to be contended with are known, with the exception only of two or three days' march beyond the limit of our late expedition."

On this and other matters, King was a visionary of sorts. He argued that the most practical way of finding the Northwest Passage safely, cheaply, and expeditiously was by overland travel with a small party of men and native guides. Larger parties with bigger boats required too much time and food, he contended. By setting up a winter camp on the Thelon River, and then finding a tributary that ran north to the Great Fish, King proposed to the Royal Society that 200 miles (320 km) of slow river and lake travel to the Arctic coast could be avoided. All that was really required, in addition, was an experienced leader, preferably someone who could also attend to the medical problems of the men; in short, a man not unlike himself.

*Augustus (Tattanneuk) served as an interpreter for John Franklin on his overland expeditions.*

For all the insights that this twenty-five-year-old possessed, he lacked the diplomacy of a Franklin to keep his criticisms to himself and the tact of a Parry to promote his ideas quietly behind closed doors. He was also rude and arrogant, as his submission to the Royal Society indicates: "The question has been asked, how can I anticipate success in an undertaking which has baffled a Parry, a Franklin and a Back?" he asked facetiously. It was not the kind of question that an organization that saw Parry and Franklin as heroes and respected Back as a former governor and founding member of its association appreciated. Nevertheless, the Society considered King's proposal, primarily because the young surgeon had, as Arthur Dobbs had a century before him, made such a public fuss and won over, as a consequence, a variety of influential individuals and newspapers.

Another time, and in another country, King might have eventually got the response that he had been seeking from the Royal Society. But apart from his own lack of tact and diplomacy and having the likes of Back and Franklin against him, he was, as historian Hugh Wallace points out, the center of a struggle between youth and age. In this case, the struggle revolved around John Barrow, now knighted and, at age seventy-two, as loyal as ever to the eighteenth-century attitudes towards the search for a northwest passage. King's plan was, in effect, of doubtful interest to the navy. More importantly, if it turned out that he was right, it would be a refutation of the existence of the kind of navigable passage that Barrow and the navy had hoped so much for.

The ensuing years for King must have been difficult ones, for while he was forced to stay at home in England to practise medicine and to play out his fight with the Admiralty in the public arena, others were successfully employing his ideas on the Arctic coast. Between 1837 and 1839, Hudson's Bay Company men Peter Warren Dease and Thomas Simpson employed the guiding services of Ouligbuck and made it all the way to Point Barrow. It was the first time the

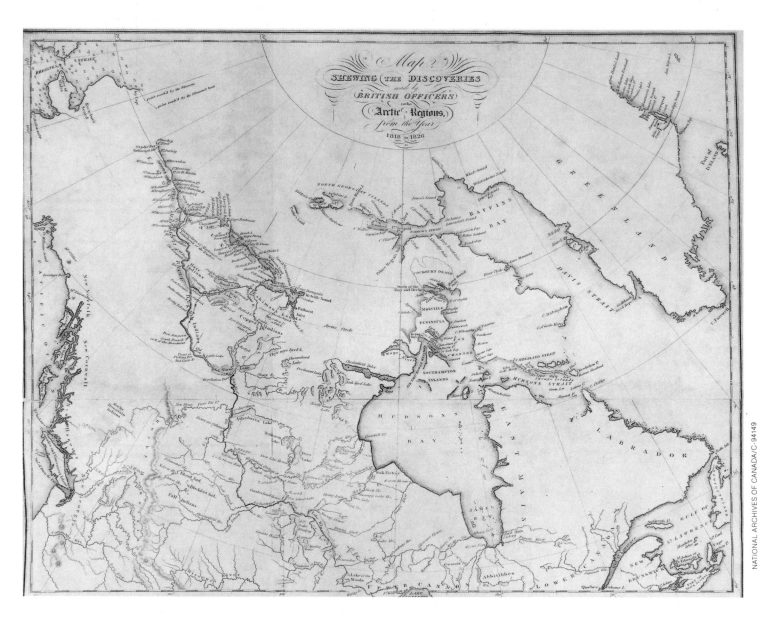

NATIONAL ARCHIVES OF CANADA/C-94149

*Arctic discoveries made by British officers between 1818 and 1826.*

Canadian Arctic coastline had been joined on the map with the western ocean. Later on, the two headed eastward, passing Franklin's Point Turnagain before reaching Montreal Island at the mouth of the Back River. From there, they went on to survey the south coast of Victoria and King William islands. Then Simpson got within reach of Cape Felix at the north end of King William Island. However, he returned unaware that James Clark Ross had erected a six-foot cairn of stones there nine years earlier. Inside it was a canister containing a message that expressed Ross's regrets at having been unable to continue on to Point Turnagain.

Simpson left the Arctic in 1839 with the false impression that King William was connected to the Boothia. It was a mistake he surely would have corrected on the next journey that he proposed. When no answer to the proposal was forthcoming from the Company's directors in England, Simpson headed back on his own to make a personal plea, unaware that the letter of approval was already on its way. Simpson never got a chance to read it, however, as he was murdered under mysterious circumstances on the trip back.

By 1844, the stage had been set for one last attempt to find the Northwest Passage. Virtually the entire Arctic coastline had been mapped, and it was evident that there was clear sailing from King William's Land to Point Barrow. Since Parry had mapped a parallel channel to the north from Baffin Bay to Melville Island, all that remained was to find the north-south channel that linked them. One more overland trek almost certainly would have solved the mystery. But Sir John Barrow, sensing victory was finally at hand, was not going to be denied. The vehicle for British discovery and the building of the empire had always been the ship, he believed, not the canoe and moccasins. If only for the pride of England, he saw no reason to break from this tradition. The Royal Geographical Society was not about to disagree.

Not surprisingly, eighteenth-century ideas of how to find the final link in the Northwest Passage also influenced the Admiralty's choice of the man to lead the expedition. Fresh from a successful Antarctic journey, James Clark Ross would have been the logical candidate, but he had indicated that he would not accept such a commission and had suggested, instead, John Franklin. Franklin had also just returned to England with his second wife, Jane Griffin, from Van Diemen's Land where he had been governor. Nearing fifty-nine years of age, overweight, and not in the best of health or spirit, Franklin became the popular choice, based more on sentiment than on careful consideration.

The decision to send Franklin, however, was little more than an afterthought for Barrow, who seemed to take no notice of the fears expressed by Back and Edward Sabine, a contemporary of Parry's, that Franklin was perhaps too old for the task. After all, Barrow must have thought, Franklin would have Britain's best sailors and two big ships, the 340-ton (308 400 kg) *Erebus* and the 370-ton (335 700 kg) *Terror*, backing him up. In addition, nothing had been spared for the voyage.

There were mixed emotions on May 19, 1845 when the *Erebus* and *Terror* sailed down the Thames River. On the one hand, Barrow declared that "there can be no objection with regard to apprehension of the loss of ships or men." On the other, Richard King, as prickly as ever, predicted that the expedition would come to be a "lasting blot in the annals of history." It didn't take long to discover who was right. Franklin and his men were last seen alive when whalers spotted them on July 26, 1845. They were tethered to an iceberg in Baffin Bay, waiting for the ice to clear from Lancaster Sound.

*A pingo rises out of wet lowlands south of the hamlet of Tuktoyaktuk on the Beaufort Sea coast. These ice-cored hills are favorite denning sites for wolves and barren-ground grizzlies.*

*Bathurst Inlet in the Central Arctic as seen from the air. An extension of Coronation Gulf, it was named by John Franklin for the third earl of Bathurst.*

# PASSAGE LANDSCAPES

*The northwest coast of Devon Island near Bear Bay. First sighted in 1616 by William Baffin, the island was named by William Edward Parry for Devon, England.*

*Opposite:*

Cumberland Sound, a large inlet on the eastern coast of Baffin Island, was explored by John Davis on his first voyage in 1585.

*Right:*

The north coast of Baffin Island's Brodeur Peninsula is a rugged rock-strewn landscape. The countless bays and fiords of the island, the fifth largest in the world, confused early explorers searching for a passage to the Orient.

*Below:*

The castellated cliffs of Elwin Inlet off Admiralty Inlet. The latter inlet, named by William Edward Parry during his exploration in 1821–23 of the west coast of Baffin Island, is one of the longest fiords in the world.

"The rude Indian canoe hauleth those seas, the Portuguese, the Saracens, and Moors travel continually up and down that reach from Japan to China, from China to Malacca, from Malacca to the Moluccas: and shall an Englishman, better appointed than any of them all (that I say no more of our navy) fear to sail in that ocean?"

—Mr. Richard Willes, English Merchant (*circa* 1575)

# 4.

# THE ADMIRALTY
# AND THE ART OF
# NEGATIVE DISCOVERY

*Ice in Lancaster Sound breaking up in late July. The ice in these waters prevented many early explorers from finding the Northwest Passage.*

The air is occasionally dead calm at the north end of Banks Island. When it is hot and humid, as it often is in mid-July, a rolling thunder can be heard in the distance, while thick, smoky fog approaches ominously from the Arctic Ocean. From a hilltop overlooking the ice in Mercy Bay, one can hear, but not always see, sandhill cranes. Their staccato, bugle-like calls echo through a small river canyon nearby, betraying their anxiety at the slightest hint of intrusion. Wherever there are sandhill cranes, there are usually muskoxen as well. The tall, long-legged birds, which migrate thousands of miles from equatorial marshes, follow in the path of these woolly survivors of the last ice age.

Like the cranes and the muskoxen, nearly everything on Banks Island, and indeed everything throughout the Arctic Archipelago, is a composite of contradistinctions that confuse and conspire against those who see only through the eyes and experiences of a nineteenth-century English explorer — the few footsteps that divide the frosty air along the ice-edge from the stifling heat of the hilltops on a hot summer's day; the grey, ice-scoured gravel beaches, which give rise to thin stems of delicate poppies, clumps of yellow potentilla, and fragrant bouquets of purple Jacob's-ladder; and, most puzzling of all, the light-refracted mirages of ghostly ships plying the smooth, icy surface of the distant Arctic Ocean.

It all must have tantalized and tortured Robert McClure in the autumn of 1852 when, desperate for a sign — another ship, a sledging party, or a break in

83

sharp in peacetime, and to continue to prove to the world, as had been done during the Napoleonic Wars, that the Royal Navy was among the greatest in the world. Just how intensely Barrow believed this is reflected in his response in 1817 to rumors of Russian exploration in the Pacific Northwest. "It would be somewhat mortifying if a naval power but of yesterday," he wrote in the *Quarterly Review*, "should complete a discovery in the nineteenth century which was so happily commenced by Englishmen in the sixteenth."

Scoresby's meeting with Barrow in 1817 to discuss the possibility of his involvement in the Admiralty's search for the Northwest Passage was thus destined to be an unhappy one. Out of respect for Joseph Banks, England's most prominent patron of natural history, Barrow had, up until that fateful occasion, pretended to be interested in Scoresby's participation. During the meeting, however, he evaded all attempts by Scoresby to pin him down, and when the whaler finally put the question directly to him, Barrow "answered shortly and indirectly," and said that, if he wished to go, he would have to take his proposals to the Navy Board the following day. No doubt, Barrow was, at the time, certain that the Navy Board's response would be a negative one, for it was he who helped devise the policy that only naval officers could be leaders of such expeditions.

As deluded as Barrow may have been about what it took to find the Northwest Passage, he had no difficulty determining what needed to be done to win the support of the public, a necessary prerequisite for any successful national plan requiring significant financing. Barrow's strategy in this respect was simple but effective. In an effort to appeal to British nationalism and to the adventuresome spirit of the Victorian armchair traveler, he set out to make this peacetime endeavor as glorious a vehicle for British honor and prestige as the wars with Napoleon had been a few years earlier. Barrow was instrumental in convincing Parliament to extend the prize of £15,000 for discovery of the Northwest Passage to the navy's captains and their crews, who had been ineligible for it up until then. He also made sure that newspapers were carefully briefed about various aspects of the expeditions and encouraged the explorers themselves to discuss openly the difficulties they had encountered. In short, no detail for promoting these ventures was spared so long as they conformed to Barrow's own carefully designed plans and ideas.

Barrow's public relations campaign ranks as one of the most successful in early nineteenth-century Britain, especially when one considers the initial miserable failures of Buchan and Franklin in trying to find the open polar sea in 1819–22 and John Ross's retreat after running up against a mythical chain of mountains the same year. In spite of these setbacks, Barrow was able to maintain the support of the public, right through to 1845, when Franklin and his men disappeared, and after.

For this, Barrow had Sir William Edward Parry to thank. The son of a prosperous doctor who had important social connections, Parry had been involved in the Admiralty's search for the passage from the beginning and participated in four expeditions in less than a decade to find it. But it was his voyage in 1819–20 that set the tone for the future, and effectively sealed the fate of Franklin and many of those, like McClure, who went out searching for him. By the standard of the time, Parry's voyage was a significant achievement. With his return to England in 1820, he and his crew had sailed through Lancaster Sound, proved that Ross's Croker Mountains did not exist, and

*The tendency of explorers to depict scenes in a picturesque way is illustrated in this sketch, The Crews of H.M.S.* Hecla *and* Griper *Cutting into Winter's Harbour, September 20, 1819. The artist shows a winding channel much like a stream in England. In reality, Parry's men would have cut a straight line in the ice.*

mapped nearly 800 miles (1290 km) of new coastline through the Arctic Archipelago. In the process, they earned the £5000 parliamentary prize as the first ship to pass 110 degrees west within the Arctic Circle, crossed Melville Island by foot, and came within a few hundred miles of reaching clear sailing to the Pacific via Prince of Wales Strait and the Beaufort Sea. The expedition was also the first to over-winter above the Arctic Circle in the Canadian North.

Not surprisingly, Parry's recipe for success was the one upon which other explorers would model their expeditions. Yet, the "Parry School," as it would come to be known, was ultimately the wrong one, for instead of operating on the principle that a viable northwest passage might not exist and proceeding cautiously with that in mind, it brazenly advocated forging ahead blindly into the Arctic Archipelago on the assumption that a passage would be found along the way.

Parry's methods were also questionable; instead of adapting to the Arctic environment, as Scoresby, for example, had advocated and as the overland expeditions of Franklin and many Hudson's Bay Company men had done, he attempted to live as he might have done back in England, impervious to the hostile environment that surrounded him. There were, to be sure, some concessions: the requisite war on dampness, ensuring a steady diet (which included the cultivation of mustard and cress) to combat scurvy, and the institution of a regular exercise regime—all these were pursued with the health of the crew in mind. But, at the same time, there was no serious thought of exploiting fresh game or fish to replace the standard fare of salted pork. Nor was there any attempt to build snow houses in the protected lee of a cliff as an alternative to holing up in a drafty ship's cabin.

In fact, so diligent were Parry's explorers in maintaining some semblance of their usual lives that an inordinate amount of time was spent staging plays, publishing newspapers, and for those who could not read or write, attending school. Parry himself uttered the disinterest with which he and his crew seemed to regard the outside world. "Not an object was to be seen on which the eye could long rest with pleasure, unless when directed to the spot where the ships lay, and where our little colony was planted," he wrote. "The smoke which there issued from several fires, affording a certain indication of the presence of man, gave a partial cheerfulness to this part of the prospect; and the sound of voice, which, during the cold weather, could be heard at a much greater distance than usual, served now and then to break the silence that reigned around us, a silence far different from that peaceable composure which characterizes the landscape of a cultivated country; it was the deathlike stillness of the most dreary desolation, and the total absence of animated existence."

In spite of many flattering biographies, Parry's stature was in large part a product of Barrow's manipulations. British historian A.E.G. Jones suggests that, in reality, Parry was a very ordinary officer, a mediocre scientist, and one inclined to nervous instability. His polar appointment, he adds, was likely the result of nepotism, for in being assigned to Ross's expedition in 1818, he had been just over halfway up the lieutenants' list and almost entirely inexperienced in cold climate navigation. Moreover, it has been suggested with justification that he conspired with Barrow to humiliate and ostracize John Ross over the Croker Mountain affair. With Parry's help, for example, Barrow helped popularize the image of a cowardly Ross conjuring up the Crokers so he would have an excuse to turn back. But the Crokers in reality had been seen by at least five other men on the expedition. And as John Ross himself later stated, if Parry had any doubts about the Croker Mountains, he was duty-bound to communicate to him. This he never did.

Parry in fact sailed as far as he did only because the winds and ice conditions in Lancaster Sound allowed him to do so. And the semblance of order, efficiency, and harmony that came to characterize his expedition prevailed in the mind of the public only because of Barrow's unscrupulous censorship of certain details in the published narrative. The fact that the public was kept unaware of the seamier side of the voyage—the death of a sailor from alcoholism, the infighting among officers, the floggings (although infrequent), and the near burning of the ship as a result of ineptitude—might not have mattered a great deal if the "gentle suppression of these images," as Barry Lopez points out, "did not foreshadow a pattern." In truth, the narratives of Parry, and others who followed, were designed largely to serve a purpose, to bolster Britain's view of the sublime Arctic landscape and the manner in which the Royal Navy pursued its search for a northwest passage through it.

By maintaining this charade and relying almost exclusively on explorers from the so-called Parry School, a pattern did emerge, and it was one for which the Admiralty had to pay a high price. Parry failed twice more after 1820 in attempts to find the Northwest Passage and left one of his ships wrecked on the shores of Somerset Island; Franklin avoided catastrophe on

Inukshuit, *once used as markers or to drive caribou towards hidden hunters, stand outside the hamlet of Igloolik in Foxe Basin. Thomas Button was the first European to visit the area and William Edward Parry wintered here.*

both of his overland expeditions; and George Back was fortunate to bring home the *Terror* on his voyage to Hudson Bay in 1837. To be sure, not everyone was unaware of what was going on. "It may doubtless gratify the national vanity to plant the standard of England even upon the sterile regions," said the *Edinburgh Review* in 1837, but "if no advantage can be gained by visiting such inhospitable regions, it must be admitted that mere knowledge of their existence, and the indentation of their shores, is comparatively useless, and utterly unworthy of that sacrifice or risk of life and resources which it may have acquired." So accepting was the British public of Barrow's misguided genius that all the negative aspects of the navy's long, painful search, all the inevitable clashes between myth and reality were never really acknowledged.

This blinkered view of Arctic exploration extended to the second generation of naval explorers, which included McClure. It also largely accounts for the chain of events that resulted in the *Investigator*'s unfortunate predicament in Mercy Bay and the bizarre occurrences that followed. In the navy since the age of seventeen, McClure was educated in the "Parry School," as a mate on George Back's *Terror* in 1836–37, and as first mate on James Clark Ross's expedition in search of Franklin in 1848. There was, however, nothing in McClure's performance on either of these voyages, nor at any other point in his career, that warranted his being given command of his own ship.

McClure's is among the most intriguing of the second generation of Northwest Passage explorations not only because it so closely followed the Parry formula, but also because it reflected the extremes to which both

Barrow and the Northwest Passage explorers would go in making the dreams and aspirations of finding the passage come true. It was also there on Mercy Bay's gravel beaches, far removed from the possibility of Inuit and Indian guides stepping in at the last minute, as they had done so often before to save the day, that English explorers' illusions about conquering the Northwest Passage would dissolve when confronted with the ultimate environmental reality of the situation.

Many historians, however, have been reluctant to portray McClure as anything but a hero. His command of the *Investigator*, for example, has been characterized as courageous, although perhaps overly enterprising at times. He has been described as selfish, reserved, and aloof in his treatment of his subordinates, but those same historians have intimated that these traits were to be expected of a British naval officer of high social rank. His accomplishments —the completion, on foot, of the passage, with relatively few deaths (five) despite four years in the Arctic—were what counted, they suggested, not how he reached his goals.

But there was a darker side to McClure, as painted by his surgeon, Alexander Armstrong, and by his interpreter, the Moravian missionary Johann Miertsching who was fluent in Inuktitut, that demonstrates just how poor a choice McClure was to command an Arctic ship and how badly the Parry formula stood up to the test of time. These accounts reveal a man with a pathological, reckless passion to be the first to navigate a passage through the Arctic. And nothing, including the health of his men, the safety of the ship, and the sublime terror of the Arctic, was permitted to stand in the way.

Almost from the start of the expedition, in 1850, McClure behaved in a manner that suggests he was determined to set his own course. When, for example, the *Investigator* sailed into Honolulu harbor, McClure was furious to discover that his commander, Richard Collinson, had set sail in the *Enterprise* northwards to the Bering Sea twenty-four hours earlier. There was really nothing particularly strange about this as the two ships had been previously appointed to rendezvous in the Bering Sea. Collinson had simply assumed that the other ship would eventually catch up. But a disturbing thought evidently crossed McClure's mind. If Collinson reached Cape Lisburne, the appointed rendezvous point, ahead of him, would he wait as they had planned or might he decide to take Commander Thomas Moore of the *Plover*, who was already stationed off the coast of Alaska, into the western Arctic and leave McClure with the "inglorious" task of standing watch in Kotzebue Sound? McClure was not one to take chances. He immediately cut short the shore leave, recalled his crew, who were out on a drunken binge, and set sail, without waiting for all of the planned-for provisions to arrive.

McClure's strategy to overtake Collinson would have alarmed even the boldest member of the Admiralty. Instead of following the prescribed route by way of the Kamchatka Peninsula, he chose a short-cut through the Aleutian Islands, a route he had heard about second-hand from a Yankee sea merchant. The infamous Aleutian fog lived up to its reputation, restricting the view from the *Investigator* to no more than a ship's length in any direction for a week at a time. McClure himself was in a frenzy throughout, as the powerful currents in the shoal-filled waters drove the ship backwards and sideways in such a disorienting manner that, at times, neither McClure nor his navigator knew where they were.

The fact that fortune rather than seamanship helped the *Investigator* get to the appointed rendezvous at Cape Lisburne did not deter McClure from pushing his luck even farther. There was no sign of the *Enterprise* there, nor had Commander Moore or Captain Henry Kellett of the warship *Herald*, whom McClure had met along the way, seen any trace of it. McClure instinctively turned to Kellett, his senior in the chain of command, for advice. Kellett's response seemed sensible: wait for a few days to see if Collinson and the *Enterprise* turned up. After all, he reasoned, by sailing through the Aleutians, McClure had cut twenty days from a voyage that would have taken Collinson fifty.

If one is to believe Dr. Armstrong, McClure deliberately deceived Kellett so that he could forge an independent course and avoid the possibility of playing second fiddle to Collinson. McClure, he suggests, pretended to be unsure that Collinson had not taken the same shortcut he had, and had not already proceeded north ahead of him. No one on board, the surgeon adds, believed this for a minute, although not one among them was unhappy that the ship was now venturing off on its own. After all, they were now taking the lead rather than settling for a supporting role in a major play that most of the people back home in Great Britain were watching. Even though Kellett twice tried to signal the *Investigator*, McClure ignored him and left. On August 1, 1850, in the comfort of 70°F (21°C) temperatures and a calm wind, he set sail for the Arctic Ocean.

In exploring the Arctic in the nineteenth century, the English explorers drew their strength from a perception of the world that gave undue credence to Isaac Newton's view of a basic harmony between man and nature. McClure's journey to Mercy Bay proved that this view, born on the hills and dales of Great Britain, was not so readily transferrable to the barren, fog-shrouded gravel beaches of the North American Arctic.

Most daunting was the power of the ice. The English believed that a good captain and disciplined crew could somehow outwit and out-muscle nature in overcoming this formidable obstacle, the unfavorable experiences of Parry, Back, Lyon, John Ross, and James Clark Ross notwithstanding. McClure, as a result, boldly pushed towards the ice-edge once he got beyond Cape Bathurst in the Beaufort Sea, and followed it northwards through Prince of Wales Strait. Managing to get within 80 miles (129 km) of Melville Island, he encountered a more threatening floe of heavy ice, "appallingly rapid" in its motion, piling in from the north.

McClure might have done the sensible thing and retreated to a safe harbor at this point, but such was his confidence in his own ability and that of the ship to triumph over nature that he pressed ahead. But the ice in Prince of Wales Strait wasn't as accommodating as the fog in the Aleutians had been. The pack kept pressing into the strait. Eventually the *Investigator* became trapped among the floes, frozen and vulnerable in the middle of the ice-choked sea. "For seventeen hours," wrote Miertsching, describing just one of the horrific scenes that the *Investigator* faced, "we stood ready on the deck where each moment appeared to be our last. Great massive pieces of ice, three and four times the size of the ship, were pushed one on top of another, and under continuing pressure, forced into a towering heap."

Through it all, the *Investigator* was tossed from one broadside to the other, until the tarred oakum began to fall out of its seams. Some of the crew were so convinced of the ship's imminent break-up that they pillaged the

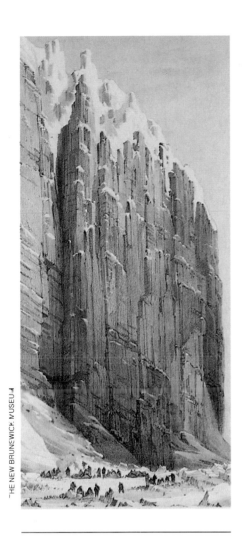

*The Bivouac, Cape Seppings, Leopold Island* was drawn by Lieutenant Browne, who accompanied James Clark Ross on his 1848–49 expedition in search of Franklin. The drawing shows a large party of sailors having dinner in May, 1848.

liquor-storage room one evening and drank themselves into a stupor, believing that they would never live to pay for their actions. Fortunately, the ship survived the ordeal once the ice froze fast and halted the destructive movement of the floes.

McClure might well have retreated home the following spring had it not been for a sledging journey he and five men had undertaken up Prince of Wales Strait that autumn. Just 25 miles (40 km) from Melville Sound, in the early hours of a cold October morning, McClure had climbed a 600-foot (183-m) promontory (Mount Observation) and waited for the sun to rise. When it did, the "long-sought-for" Northwest Passage lay before him, with the north coast of Banks Island visible to the west and Parry's Viscount Melville Sound stretching to the east.

McClure's intention was to press through Prince of Wales Strait when the warm weather eventually freed the *Investigator* from the ice in spring. But that was not meant to be. Nine months later, the ship was still fixed as fast in the ice as it had been during the coldest part of winter. And when, in mid-August, the ship was finally able to press some distance northward, it was abruptly blocked by "great island-like masses" that had been driven down by the currents and the north winds. The captain apparently then made up his mind to turn south and circumnavigate Banks Island in the hope of reaching what is today known as McClure Strait. Some of the crew misinterpreted the change in course as a retreat to the Bering Sea.

Once again, McClure found the ice a formidable adversary, especially as he steered the *Investigator* northward along the west coast of the island. With "frightful polar ice" on the west side of the ship, and a high shoreline on the east side, the open-water channel eventually became so narrow that the crew members could almost touch the rocks on one side and the ice on the other. "For two hours we sailed along this narrow channel where projecting angles of the heaped-up ice masses often had to be blasted away before the ship could pass," wrote Miertsching. "Then we came to a regular ice-labyrinth which brought the ship to a full stop." Here was the true polar ice, of which Miertsching stated, "No one can form a conception without actually seeing it." To describe it, he said, "One must write archives full, and then those who have seen only European ice in rivers, ponds, and the sea would find it unintelligible and beyond belief."

That may have well been the end of the *Investigator*, as the "pitiless" ice squeezed the ship with such violence that it was thrust onto its left side, then onto its right. The frozen masses piled up so high that they threatened to come tumbling down and crush the ship. "This is the end," McClure himself admitted at one point. "The ship is breaking up; in five minutes she will be sunk!" In a "trembling" voice, McClure gave the order to cut the cables, so that the ship would be driven onto shore, where it could at least continue to provide food and shelter. Before the fateful act could be carried out by the crew, however, a dramatic change developed in their precarious situation. "In the most awful moment of our lives," writes Miertsching, "the ice became silent and motionless. This memorable moment was almost too much for us; each man rested against the bulwarks of the listing ship, and pale and trembling all over, stared at his comrade who stared back at him; not a sound or word could be heard, so that on the ship there reigned a death-like calm." Miraculously, the *Investigator* was set free, allowing McClure to continue

*Critical Position of H.M.S. Investigator on the North Coast of Baring (Banks) Island, August 20, 1851 by Samuel G. Cresswell, an artist on Robert McClure's voyage in search of Franklin.*

steering in a northerly direction. Rounding Cape Prince Alfred, the ship headed eastward until it arrived at Mercy Bay. On September 23, 1851, the water passage to the east through Viscount Melville Sound was still relatively clear of ice. But McClure, perhaps weary of taking any more chances, had other ideas. Instead of pushing ahead, as might have been expected, he dispatched Stephen Court, the ship's Second Master, to check the depth of Mercy Bay. He then anchored the *Investigator* there to make preparation for the winter, thinking that he could easily complete the voyage the following spring. "It was the 'fatal error of our voyage,'" said an embittered Dr. Armstrong in his own narrative. "This opinion I formed at the time, personally expressed it, and recorded it in my Journal; therefore, I could not be, in any degree, influenced by subsequent events: and, that the decision then arrived at, of entering this bay, was a hasty one, was fully established by its results."

For the crew of the *Investigator* that second winter came quickly to Mercy Bay. By the end of September, there were already 6 inches (15 cm) of ice around the ship, and the temperature was bitingly cold—dipping to −4°F (−20°C) at night and rising to no more than 8°F (−13°C) during the day. (By winter, it would often plummet to −51°F [−46°C]). As the days shortened, until there was no light at all, a regular winter routine developed. To keep things dry, the crew stoked up the stoves with coal and laid red-hot cannon balls on the lower deck. But nothing could remove the dampness from their clothes and blankets. "Everything is moist and damp," Miertsching said "continuous dripping from the deck, and the beds damp through. Ah! could I only sleep one night in a dry, warm bed." McClure ordered an inventory of the

food supply and immediately put the men on two-thirds rations (he later reduced it to half) against the advice of his surgeon. For the remainder of the first winter, "truly dark and gloomy times [as] the wolves make themselves heard almost daily," the men were each given three candles a week, then three candles for fourteen days—barely enough to provide eighteen hours of light.

*Observing through a sextant* (left) *and Arctic clothing of the Franklin era* (above), *as depicted in* Illustrated Arctic News *in the 1850s.*

If McClure is to be given any credit, it was for his willingness to exploit the fresh game around him. Perhaps he got the idea from John Ross, who attributed his survival and the survival of all but one of his men between 1829 and 1833 to the consumption of fresh meat that the Inuit recommended to him. For the crew of the *Investigator*, however, this strategy served not only to augment the diminishing food supply but also to improve the health of the men (although many complained of having to eat fresh caribou and muskoxen in place of two-year-old salted pork); it also boosted morale by temporarily relieving the monotony of life aboard the frozen ship. After a day-long hunt, the weary hunters returned to their sleeping-quarters with colorful tales of their pursuits. One man, upon returning to the ship empty-handed, explained that he had shot three legs off a hare but, after pursuing the animal for two hours and then shooting the fur off its side, it had managed to get away "half-naked."

Altogether, the men of the *Investigator* killed 7 muskoxen, 110 caribou, 169 hares, 186 grouse, 198 ducks, 29 geese, 2 wolves, and 4 polar bears during two-year ordeal in Mercy Bay. Yet, by the second winter their (their third in the Arctic), dozens of the crew had been confined to their beds, suffering from physical or mental illness brought on by hunger, largely because of McClure's determination to extend the food supply long enough for the ship to break free. Those crew members who were fit enough could be seen, almost daily, scrounging through the garbage heaps, looking for some rotting morsels. Lieutenant Robert Wyniatt had become so crazed and despondent at one point that he often howled all night long, despite the protestations of his fellow shipmates. On one occasion, he had to be lowered to the ice, screaming, after threatening three times to murder McClure.

Like Barrow, the leaders of these Northwest Passage expeditions were not adverse to presenting details of their journeys in the most favorable light. Parry, for example, had written the accounts of his second journey during the inactive part of the winter on the assumption that it would be the only story told to the public. To his great annoyance, Alexander Fisher, the assistant surgeon, kept a duplicate journal, which he did not hand in and later pub-

*Water carriers* (above) *and tumbling on the ice* (right).

lished. McClure acted no differently than Parry had. Although he could be, as both Armstrong and Miertsching had demonstrated, callously indifferent to the sufferings of his men, this sort of behavior was never even hinted at in his own narrative. For example, he makes no mention of ordering three of the half-starved crew flogged for stealing the dogfood set aside for the ship's mascot, Mango. And while Wyniatt was in the throes of a deep psychosis and Dr. Armstrong was pleading for more food for the men, McClure's narrative merely stated that "there is, for the most part, a contented state of mind" and that hunger had not caused any increase in disease "except that those of a very nervous temperament became easily excited and unreasonable."

McClure must have understood just how desperate the situation was, for in September 1852, he assembled the crew and announced a truly sinister plan for escape the following spring, one that would surely have sent most or all of those assigned to certain death. The idea was to dispatch two parties in separate directions. The first group, led by Lieutenant William Haswell, included poor Wyniatt and twelve of the sickest men. They were to travel east 500 miles (805 km) over the ice to Port Leopold, where, in 1848, James Clark Ross had cached some food and clothing and left a small steamboat. (McClure had no proof that the supplies were still there.) At Port Leopold, the group would wait to be picked up by a whaling vessel and returned to England. A second, smaller party of ten, four of whom were already confined to their beds and barely able to climb to the ship's deck, were to travel with Lieutenant Samuel Cresswell, the expedition's artist, and Miertsching. They were to retreat south on foot overland to the Princess Royal Islands in Prince of Wales Strait, then set out by boat past Wollaston Land (Victoria Island), cross Dolphin and Union Strait, go across to the Mackenzie River and up to Fort Good Hope. With the help of Indians, they were to travel across the wilds of North America to Montreal and New York. McClure decided that he, the ship's surgeon, and the healthiest of the men would spend one more winter aboard the *Investigator*. And if help was not forthcoming by the end of it, they would set off for Port Leopold as well.

McClure later explained that he was giving the men the only chance they would have to save their lives. Another winter aboard the *Investigator*, he explained, would have resulted in certain death. In reality, he was giving them no chance at all. In 1851, Leopold McClintock, with eighty days' provisions and a healthy crew, had made a round trip of 760 miles (1224 km) along almost the same route that Haswell was to take. In contrast, Haswell was to receive forty-five days' allowance to complete the journey. The second group under Cresswell were to receive food for only thirteen days. Although McClure had at the time known nothing of McClintock's sledging trip, he did know that Cresswell had spent thirty-four days in the first year of their Arctic journey on a trip that was shorter than the one that he was now expected to complete in just thirteen days, and with a group of desperately ill men, one of whom couldn't be made to understand that he was leaving the ship while another had to be "handled like an idiot child." Even Miertsching, who respected McClure, had trouble fathoming the sanity of the plan as the time of departure drew near. "Twenty-one men are now in hospital and in six weeks, we must, with those judged unfit to remain longer with the ship, harness ourselves to sledges laden with supplies, and drag them through snow and ice for hundreds of miles. How many of us will in this way see Europe? The answer is: 'No one.'"

Months later, in April 1853, just a week before McClure planned to launch this desperate scheme, an event comparable to Stanley's famous encounter with Livingstone unfolded. At the moment the captain was morosely telling Miertsching that, if he didn't see him the following year in Europe, he could be assured that he would be dead, unburied, and wrapped in the fur coat that Miertsching had given him, McClure spotted a black object moving towards the ship in the distance. Assuming at first that it might be a muskoxen, then an Inuk, McClure soon found himself confronted by a man, "whose face was as black as ebony." It turned out to be Lieutenant Bedford Pim of Kellett's ship *Resolute*. Pim had sledged over from Dealy Island where the *Resolute* had wintered and discovered a note in a cairn left by McClure the previous autumn. The note outlined the *Investigator*'s predicament and location.

"It was first pronounced either a mistake or a joke," Dr. Armstrong said in describing the reaction of the crew to Pim's arrival. "Indeed, the mind for a moment appeared confused, as if unable to comprehend the truth of what was heard.... At length when thoroughly aroused by a shout of joy raised by the few men on deck, announcing the approach of the stranger, there was a sudden rush to the hatchways; the weak and the strong "the maimed, the halt, and the blind" following each other, amazed and agitated, as fast as their enfeebled limbs could bear them. It was unquestionably an emotional moment for Pim as well. When he saw the half-starved crew sitting down to breakfast the morning of his arrival—"a cup of weak cocoa without sugar and a moiety of bread"—he rushed to his sledge on the ice and brought back a large piece of bacon—"the only breakfast we had known for many a long day," said Armstrong.

Pim's timely arrival, however, did nothing to temper the pathological side of McClure. Still convinced that he could free the ship and complete the Northwest Passage, he refused to abandon it. Instead, with a small party of men, he sledged to Kellett's ship to discuss the matter further. He cruelly ordered the starving who had been left behind to remain on half-rations to preserve the food supply for the possibility of another winter.

One can only guess how Kellett responded to McClure's plan, given the nature of their last meeting in the Bering Sea and McClure's refusal to accept his advice. But when Kellett stood face-to-face with the decrepit invalids who arrived a short time after McClure—his answer left little doubt. Stopping short of ordering McClure to scrap his crazy plan, he sent him back with Armstrong and his own surgeon, Dr. William T. Domville. If the two surgeons found the

Robert McClure's Journey
(1850 – 54)

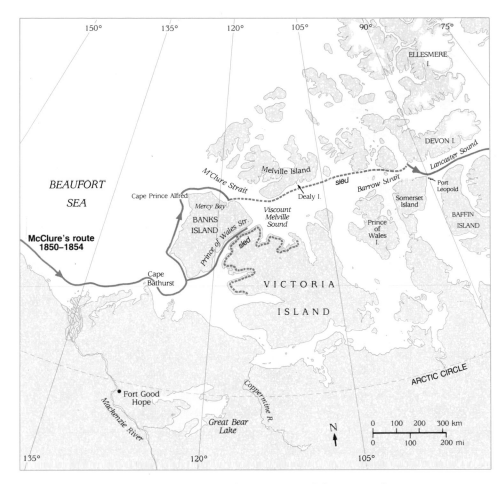

men to be fit, and if McClure could find twenty of them to volunteer to stay on, he could have his way, Kellett decided. If not, the *Investigator* was to be immediately abandoned and the crew nursed back to health before their return to England.

To no one's surprise, except McClure's, only four men volunteered, no doubt because, as British naval officers, they were duty-bound to volunteer for such missions. That McClure could have expected or even hoped for the support of so many men who had already suffered for so long is dumbfounding. Dr. Domville's testimony to a select committee of the House of Commons upon returning to England, cautious as it was, tells the story: "One man subject to periods of mental aberration; one man in a state of dementia, his condition and appearance rendered still more pitiable from severe frostbite of the fingers; two men carried on sledges, the one with scurvy, the other with urinary disease and phlegmonous inflammation of the leg; the remainder all the more or less affected with scorbutic disease and debility, as indicated to the spectator in the tottering gait, attenuated form, and care-worn expression of countenance."

The true story of the *Investigator* and McClure's conduct throughout the expedition must have been the subject of heated debate within the Admiralty and of ripe public gossip following the court-martial that was automatically called whenever a ship was abandoned. When asked by the select committee if he would consider sharing with his rescuers the prize of £10,000 that he was entitled to for discovering the Northwest Passage (McClure was not given the full £15,000 in deference to what Franklin might have discovered should he be found), McClure produced Kellett's orders for him to abandon ship, and insisted that the *Investigator* would have been freed and the Northwest Passage found, without Kellett's help. Kellett was never called upon to respond, but, evidently appalled by the snub, he later offered to contribute £50 for a fund to compensate his crew.

As was true of other tales of Arctic ordeal, the real story largely escaped the public's attention. McClure's own official account of the trip portrayed it as heroic (it was written by Sherard Osborn, a friend and fellow naval officer) and avoids dealing with the more controversial aspects of the journey. Armstrong's indictment of McClure, which was published two years later, was largely overlooked or dismissed by some historians as biased because of the surgeon's intense dislike for the captain. As for Miertsching, his more balanced recollections of the journey weren't published in English for another century.

During the next fourteen years, during which time Franklin's fate would be conclusively determined, the Admiralty's interest in Arctic exploration waned with the increasing number of failures. It spent £675,000 on the Franklin search, largely as a result of relentless public pressure brought to bear by Lady Jane Franklin. She herself raised another £35,000 and inspired the U.S. government and American shipping magnate Henry Grinnell to donate another £250,000 to the cause.

*A portrait of Lady Jane Franklin.*

All but a handful of the thirty-four ships (there were probably more, as whalers kept a watch out as well, but how many is uncertain) that were commissioned for the search up to 1858 were under the Admiralty's command. What it got in return were several near disasters and more fruitless searches. Of Sir Edward Belcher's five ships, which were sent out in 1852—the *Assistance*, under himself and Commander G.N. Richards, the steam tender *Pioneer* under Sherard Osborn, the *Resolute* under Kellett, the *Intrepid* under Leopold McClintock and the *North Star* under W.J.S. Pullen—four were abandoned in the ice, because, it seems, Belcher had no desire to stay in the Arctic another season. The *Breadalbane* under William Fawckner sunk in fifteen minutes on August 21, 1853, off Cape Riley after being crushed by ice.

Even worse was the infighting, the bickering, and the shameful lack of co-operation among ships and shipmates themselves. For example, Captain Horatio Austin, commander of a four-vessel expedition that was launched in 1850, only grudgingly accepted the Admiralty's decision to allow the accomplished whaler William Penny to join in the search for Franklin. He was, however, resolute in his determination not to go out of his way to help Penny. In the most notable of the clashes between the two, Penny asked the veteran naval officer for his steamer tender so he could push through the ice-choked waters of Wellington Channel. When he failed to get the assistance he asked for, Penny blamed Austin. Austin attributed it to a misunderstanding. The result was that the search for Franklin was prolonged, and confused. Penny was so disgusted with the whole affair that he never again volunteered his services. Charles Codrington Forsythe behaved no better. On loan from the navy to command Lady Franklin's *Prince Albert* in 1850, he could not hide his disdain for the whalers who had been selected to serve under him. "I had not a soul I could associate with without my condescension being imposed upon, nor could I leave one in charge of the vessel," he said at the time. As a result, he abandoned the search through Prince Regent Inlet at the first opportunity. Lost with his retreat was perhaps the best opportunity to find Franklin, for it was down this waterway that both of his ships had gone.

In the face of these debacles, the Admiralty responded as it had to the true story of McClure and the *Investigator*. The cowardly Belcher escaped punishment, even though two of his officers, Kellett and McClintock, were convinced that the abandonment wasn't necessary (their contentions were borne out when whalers found Kellett's empty vessel floating in the Davis Strait pack the following year). Austin was found not to be at fault by a committee of naval officers, despite the fact that Alexander Stewart, captain of the sister ship *Sophia*, had witnessed the unfortunate episode with Penny. The idea, of course, was, as always, to save face. Even in the darker moments of these Arctic endeavors, Barrow was not above trying to make a silk purse out of a sow's ear. When Forsythe returned to England in 1850 with news that relics of Franklin had been found at Beechey Island, Barrow touted it as "one of the most extraordinary voyages ever performed in the polar seas." In reality, Forsythe was simply relaying information that had been discovered by another crew.

Left behind in the wake of McClure's haste and daring, Richard Collinson arrived back in England in 1855. Having tried and failed to catch up with the *Investigator*, his *Enterprise* got as far as Cambridge Bay in 1852. There, his crew discovered part of a cabin door which almost certainly belonged to one of Franklin's missing ships. Had Collinson been able to talk to the Inuit of the area, he may have been able to trace the door's origins. Because Miertsching, the expedition's interpreter, was with McClure, however, he was never able to do so. As it was though, Collinson was so drunk while in command, and so conservative during his brief moments of sobriety, that there was little chance of him gaining any insights. At one point, his Ice Master complained so bitterly about the expedition's lack of progress in the face of so few obstacles that he proclaimed, "I am afraid to think of what we shall do if we meet with difficulty from ice. Poor Sir John [Franklin]. God help you—you'll get none from us."

It is difficult not to feel some sympathy for Collinson, however. He spent more than five years away from England, got as close to completing the Northwest Passage as McClure had, and returned with a reasonably healthy crew. The times in England had changed, however, and there would be no praise and hyperbole left from the likes of Barrow to disguise the miserable failure of the larger naval effort. Collinson as a consequence became one of the first scapegoats. So bitter was he for the manner in which he was treated that he never again applied for another Admiralty posting.

Ultimately, Barrow's notion of a northwest passage was predicated, as was the British public's, on a number of antiquated assumptions, including the idea of an open polar sea and the firm belief that a navigation of the passage could be accomplished in a single season. These illusions left those naval explorers chosen to undertake the task ill-prepared to deal with a frozen landscape that did not reveal its mysteries readily. The density of the ice caught them completely off-guard and unable to describe what they were up against. Yet, the belief in the harmony between man and nature was so strong that they forged ahead until the ice crippled their ships or sank them.

Division of Sledges Passing Cape Lady Franklin; Extraordinary Masses of Ice Pressed Against the North Shore of Bathurst Land *was sketched by Walter W. May, a lieutenant on board the H.M.S.* Assistance *under the command of Sir Edward Belcher. Like many of his fellow officers, May had a serious falling out with his commander Sir Edward Belcher.*

"Nature no longer feels her heart beat in the slumber of the north…moral nature seems to have abdicated, and nothing remains but chaos without a purpose, in which everything clashes confusedly and by chance."

—FROM THE MEMOIRS OF JOSEPH RENÉ BELLOT, 1855

# THE WRECK OF HOPE

An old Inuit tale tells of a man named Qitdlarssuaq or Qitlaq who was as renowned for his bald head, which legend suggests gave off a glow at night, as for his supernatural powers. Qitlaq, we know from his son Merqusaq, had led a group of about fifty Inuit from northern Baffin Island to Devon Island some time around 1832, to escape a blood feud. He had apparently murdered a man in an act of avenging a friend's death, and made the journey north to avoid the threat of retaliation. That he could have convinced so many people to join him attests to his shaman's powers and to his skills as a navigator. One legend tells of how he and a young companion were caught on the sea ice in a storm that broke the hard surface all around them. Faced with almost certain death from drowning or exposure, Qitlaq ordered his companion to close his eyes and to lie face down on the sled. The curiosity of the young man got the best of him, however. After he felt the sled moving, he looked up to see that Qitlaq had turned himself into a polar bear. And wherever he went, the open sea turned to ice.

As fantastic as the story sounds, the paths of Qitlaq and the British explorers searching for Franklin actually crossed in 1852 when Edward Inglefield, the commander of the *Isabel*, met him on Devon Island. Inglefield had by then surveyed the west coast of Greenland to Cape Alexander and penetrated Smith Sound before exploring Jones and then Lancaster sounds. During the encounter, he had told Qitlaq of an isolated group of Greenland Inuit living on the island's extreme northwest coast. Qitlaq "could never settle down to anything" after hearing that story, according to Merqusaq. So he

*The remains of Franklin House on Beechey Island.*

convinced his followers to make the long migration to Greenland across the ice. It was, as might be expected, a long and perilous ordeal, so daunting that partway through some of the followers despaired at ever finding the new land and turned back.

Qitlaq and his group made it to Greenland, however. They settled in the Etah area for a year before finally meeting the Greenlanders they had traveled so far to find. Evidently, it was a joyful encounter, for in co-habitating with their cousins, the Canadian Inuit reintroduced them to the lost art of kayak-construction and bow hunting, while the Greenlanders taught the Canadians the art of dovekie trapping, a unique form of catching birds in flight. But all did not end well. Qitlaq was once again driven to murder—a local shaman was his victim this time—and, as before, he avoided retribution by fleeing. With his followers trailing behind, Qitlaq headed back home across the ice in Smith Sound. But, before he made it to Devon Island, he was suddenly stricken with severe abdominal pains, and then died. (In 1987, Renee Wissink and Mike Beedell with Paul Apak and Theo Ikummaq, both descendants of Qitlaq's sister, retraced the epic journey to Greenland where the first two hunters they met were also descendants of Qitlaq.)

The story of Qitlaq and others like him highlights two things about nineteenth-century Arctic exploration that the British naval officers were slow to understand: the Inuit were explorers in their own right and they understood the Arctic landscape well enough to know how to take advantage of it. The problem, once again, was a matter of perception. Viewed by most naval officers, the Arctic landscape was barren and lifeless, an immovable barrier that could swallow or crush a big ship. There was no room for the more gentle Inuit view of the ice as merely an extension of the land, a way to get from one island in the archipelago to another, or as a bountiful source of seals, walrus, or other marine mammal life.

The British, however, could not forever ignore the expertise of the Inuit especially in light of the failure of the Franklin expedition and the inability of a large number of search parties to find him. In time, they recognized the ability of the Inuit to draw extremely detailed maps, and consulted with a number of them about the possible whereabouts of the missing men. The whaler Penny even experimented with the use of Inuit dogs and sledges in his search for Franklin. But such was the regimented nature of the Admiralty's plans in general, and the British officers' faith in their own intellectual and technical superiority, that the lessons were often ignored. The predilection of the explorers was to resort to technological advances in their own European world to bolster their hopes and prospects. So, instead of building igloos, hunting seals, and wearing fur-lined clothing or caribou skins, they used the Sylvester stove, India-rubber ground cloths, and tinned meat—all effective to some degree, but hardly a match for Inuit ingenuity and common sense.

The Hudson's Bay Company employees, on the other hand, understood the advantage of "going native," largely because of their long association with Indians and the Métis of the boreal forest. And so, while Barrow and a handful of naval officers were wrapping up preparations for the Franklin voyage in 1845, the Company was engaging in a plan for Arctic discovery as well; in this case, the intent was to continue on the Arctic coast, where Dease and Simpson had left off, with the idea of determining once and for all if Boothia was an island. If it was, the survey of the North American coastline would be

*Members of the 1987 Qitdlarssuaq expedition rest near Makinson Inlet, Ellesmere Island.*

completed and the whereabouts of the Northwest Passage would finally be solved.

The strategy of the Hudson's Bay Company was, from the outset, to travel as the Inuit did. "I am decidedly of the opinion that, the survey cannot be completed in the course of one season, & that, it will be necessary to pass either one or two winters on the voyage," said Governor George Simpson in drawing up the instructions in 1845. "It would be quite impossible to take a sufficient quantity of provisions for the maintenance of the people for so long a time, you must therefore, be prepared to winter within the Esquimaux & fare as they do."

The man the Company chose to "complete the geography of the northern shores of America" in 1845 was John Rae, a thirty-two-year-old Scottish doctor from the Orkneys who had come to work for the company years earlier. Ouligbuck, the Inuk who had traveled with Richardson, Simpson, and Dease, would go with him. He had already been involved in the charting of more coastline than anyone else, and was regarded as an essential component of the expedition party.

If there was ever a man who stood in perfect contrast to Franklin and the other naval explorers, it was Rae. In the words of one man who knew him, "he was very muscular and active, full of animal spirits, and had a fine intellectual countenance...one of the best snow-shoe walkers in the service [and] an excellent shot." Rae grew up in Scotland, climbing mountains, fishing, and relishing every opportunity to be outdoors. He could walk 100 miles (161 km) in two days and once made a 1200-mile (1932-km) return trip from the Red River colony to Sault Ste. Marie in two months. Simpson, as tough a critic as there was in the company, thought him to be the "fittest man in the country" and knew no one better than him "as regards the management of the people and the endurance of toil, either by walking, boating or starving."

The typical naval ship carried with it about 70 to 100 men, 70 tons (63 500 kg) of coal, 1455 gallons (6605 L) of rum, 21 000 pounds (9534 kg) of biscuit, 32 000 pounds (14 528 kg) of salted pork and beef, 1300 pounds (590 kg) of scotch barley, 4000 pounds (1816 kg) of chocolate, 56 000 pounds (25 424 kg) of flour, and tens of thousands of pounds of preserved meats, vegetables, barley, rice, lime juice, and tobacco. (Franklin's last expedition carried much more.) Rae's party, in contrast, comprised thirteen men, including Ouligbuck, Ouligbuck's son William, and the Cree Indian Nibitabo, whom Rae recognized as a hunter of unparalleled skill. They would have two clinker-built craft, the *North Pole* and the *Magnet*, measuring 22 feet (7 m) long, and 7.5 feet (228 cm) wide and rigged with two lug sails, each capable of carrying fifty or sixty boxes weighing 90 pounds (41 kg) each. The idea quite obviously was to keep the expedition as light as possible, and Rae was serious about it. As a non-smoker, he went so far as to leave a supply of tobacco behind at the last minute to reduce the weight. (The weight of tobacco on the *Erebus* and *Terror* alone exceeded the total lading of Rae's two boats.) Being aware also of the "injurious effects of spirits, particularly in cold climates," he would allow for only 4 gallons (18 L) of brandy and 2 gallons (9 L) of port wine.

Departing on June 13, 1846, it took Rae twenty days to reach Repulse Bay near the northwest end of Hudson Bay by boat. There, he confirmed Inuit reports that Repulse Bay was separated from the northern sea by a narrow isthmus. Rae crossed this isthmus, entered the waters he called Committee Bay, and then reluctantly returned to his landing after a brief exploration. Going home was the farthest thing from his mind, however.

Instead, he built a house of stones (Fort Hope) and set about to hunt for wild game. In October alone, Rae and his party killed 63 caribou, 5 hares, 1 seal, and 172 partridge, and caught 116 trout. Another 100 caribou would be added to the food cache the following month, giving him and his small group almost as much game as the crew of the *Investigator* was able to secure in two years. The following spring, Rae and the rest of the party completed the survey of the Gulf of Boothia, mapping 655 miles (1055 km) of new land and coastline and proving once and for all that Boothia Peninsula was not an island.

The closest Rae's correspondence comes to describing the significance of his achievements is that he confesses that it was the "most fatiguing" thing that he had ever done ("However, we marched merrily on, tightening our belts, mine came in six inches"). The journey was, of course, much more than a tough haul. Rae may not have been the first non-native explorer to truly adopt the indigenous mode of travel, but he was, as the historian E.E. Rich suggests, "the foremost practical exponent of it." As such, his would become the model upon which other successful explorers would mold their expeditions.

Leopold McClintock, the so-called father of Arctic sledging, recognized that Rae and his party were "the first white men who maintained themselves in the Arctic regions by their own unaided efforts." Recognition for Rae's achievements back home in England, however, came slowly. Part of it had to do with his modesty, but it was also because Barrow and the Admiralty had diverted almost all public attention to Franklin and to the fleet of ships it had sent out to find him.

*A large cairn on King William Island where members of Franklin's crew were sighted by Inuit.*

It would be unfair to say that the Admiralty's ships and the privately sponsored expeditions that accompanied them accomplished nothing. Nearly 40 000 miles (64 400 km) of the Arctic had been sledged in the search for Franklin by 1857, 8600 (13 850 km) of them by Leopold McClintock, George Frederick Mecham, Richard Vesey Hamilton, George Strong Nares, and Bedford Pim in the 1852 – 54 season alone. McClintock covered 1320 miles (2125 km) in 105 days; Mecham, 1328 miles (2138 km) in 84 days. Rae walked 6515 miles (10 490 km) during his four expeditions, including a 1720-mile (2770 km) hike from Fort Chipewyan to Crow Wing, Minnesota, in 54 days. As a result, a huge area, which had only fifteen years earlier been an empty space on the maps, was now charted. Even the unlikely regions of northern Baffin Bay and Smith Sound between Greenland and Ellesmere Island were searched by Inglefield and the flamboyant American Elisha Kent Kane—the latter, primarily it seems, on the pretext of reaching the mythical open polar sea through the North Water. Kane's pursuit ended in failure and probably hastened his death at thirty-seven. Nevertheless, he became a full-fledged American hero and was given a funeral procession by train from New Orleans to his birth place in Philadelphia, a tribute to his image as a hero.

Yet, despite the extravagant efforts, few clues of Franklin were found. Captain Erasmus Ommaney discovered some rope, wood, and canvas when he landed on Devon Island in 1850. This indicated that Franklin and his men had probably landed there to conduct magnetic observations. Around the same time, John Ross (since 1847, Ross had been warning the Admiralty, the Royal Society, and anyone else who would listen that the Franklin crews were in trouble, but his calls for a search failed, primarily because the Admiralty didn't want another expedition frozen in), Edwin De Haven, Samuel Griffin, William Penny, and William Stewart converged on Beechey Island to the west. One of their landing parties discovered the graves of three men who had been part of the Franklin expedition (a glove was found by Captain Osborn of the *Pioneer* a few days later), but, oddly enough, no written message about their intended course was found. William Penny found the remains of a camp, including a newspaper scrap dated 1844, up the coast of Wellington Channel.

In comparison, Rae's four journeys resulted in the mapping of 625 miles (1006 km) of coastline—on the first journey, from the northwest corner of Melville Peninsula to Lord Mayor Bay—and the retracing of 1375 miles (2214 km) of coastline—on the second in 1848 with sixty-year-old John Richardson (whom he got on well with, but found his men to be the "most awkward, lazy and careless set I ever had anything to do with"). The third expedition in 1851 brought him to within 50 miles (81 km) of the *Erebus* and *Terror*, after hiking and boating along more than 620 miles (1000 km) of the Victoria Island coastline. It was on this journey's return that he found two pieces of wood—oak and pine—near the mouth of the Great Fish River. He was certain that they had come from a naval vessel—whose, he wasn't sure—but he guessed that they had probably been carried down by a southerly flowing strait that divided Victoria Island from north Somerset Island.

Rae returned to the area in 1853 – 54 and met up with an Inuk at Pelly Bay who gave him second-hand reports of the dead and starving explorers. It was a hauntingly grim end for the men of the *Erebus* and *Terror*. Some Inuit families had spotted about forty white men on King William Island, traveling south and dragging a boat and sledges behind them. Although none of the Europeans could speak Inuktitut, it was deduced that the ships had been crushed by ice, and that they were heading towards the mainland to find caribou. Apparently the Inuit didn't see them alive again but, later in the season, in the area of Montreal Island at the mouth of the Great Fish River, they found their bodies scattered about.

"From the mutilated state of many of the bodies and the contents of the kettle," Rae was to report back to his employers in London, "it is evident that our wretched Countrymen had been driven to the last dread alternative, as a means of sustaining life. A few of the unfortunate Men must have survived until the arrival of the wild fowl (say, until the end of May), as shots were heard, and fresh bones and feathers of geese were noticed near the scene of the sad event."

The mysterious fate of Franklin was all but confirmed. But instead of being lionized for the discovery, Rae was pilloried in public. It was the Middleton story all over again; the reality of his first-hand discovery clashed with public expectations at home. Rae's problem was that he intimated that a British citizen, no less than a naval officer, was capable of committing an act of cannibalism. Even though Rae brought back a medal, silver plate, silver spoons and forks, and other items bearing the crests of various members of the Franklin crew to give credibility to the tale, a great many people refused, or didn't want, to believe him. Both Lady Franklin and the news journals publicly doubted that civilized subjects of the King were capable of resorting to such an act, no matter how desperate the circumstances. They attributed the mutilation to wild beasts and suggested that the Inuit had killed the men for material gain. The novelist Charles Dickens wrote in *Household Words* that it was impossible for such a thing to happen. The moral improbability, he wrote, far outweighed in relative importance "the wild tales of a herd of savages."

Rae admitted that some of the Inuit reports were based on imperfect knowledge, but in a series of letters to *The Times*, he affirmed his belief in what the Inuit had told him. For that, he paid a high price. When, on behalf of the search party, he applied for the £10,000 reward for himself and his party for discovering the fate of Franklin, his employers at the Hudson's Bay Company callously decided that his pay "should remain in abeyance" until it was decided by the government whether or not he should receive the reward. It was, as he would protest, a ridiculous decision, given that his pay had nothing to do with his collection of the reward. That wasn't the only trouble he faced. More than one person maliciously suggested that he had rushed back to England to collect the reward instead of pursuing the search for Franklin. The charges were somewhat understandable because Rae's full account of what had occurred on his journey had not yet been made public. His abbreviated version, in the meantime, left a great deal to speculation.

In fact, Rae did not find out about the reward until his return to England in 1854. Furthermore, he had no reason to believe that the Inuit who told him the story knew the general location of the *Erebus* and *Terror*. The information, he says, was conveyed to him when he returned to Repulse Bay.

Rae found the ensuing controversy all "very humiliating and extremely disagreeable." He had dedicated the best part of a decade of his life to the exploration of the Arctic, and had done it more successfully and efficiently than had anyone before him. Although he was eventually given the reward, the ill-will persisted. And as deserving as he was, he was never granted a

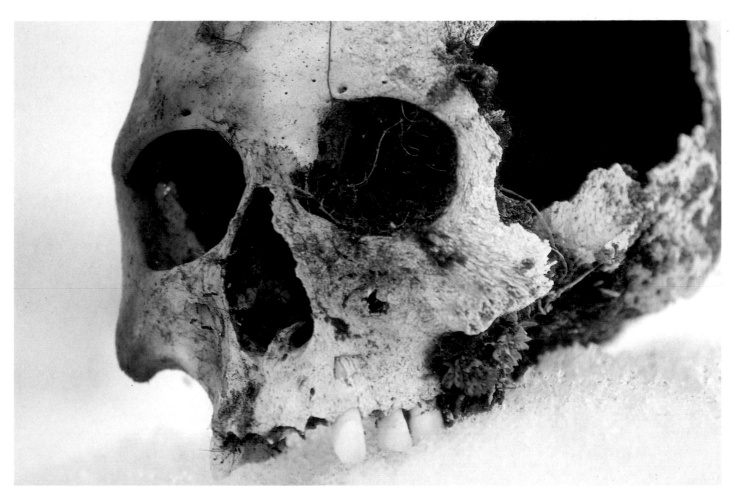

*A skull found by the photographer near the remains of an encampment on the Tasmania Islands in Franklin Strait.*

knighthood as had many of his lesser contemporaries. With Rae's return to England and the fate of Franklin largely discovered, the Admiralty was in no mood to risk more lives and money to determine the details of the Franklin tragedy. It had already lost five ships in the search for Franklin, and three more—Collinson's *Enterprise*, Rochfort Maguire's *Plover*, and Henry Trollope's *Rattlesnake*—were still somewhere in the Bering Sea or the western Arctic in 1855. In deference to Lady Franklin and public pressure, however, it called upon the Hudson's Bay Company to carry out a search down the Great Fish River—the course of action Richard King had been advocating for nearly a decade.

Rae would have been the logical choice to lead the trip; however, he turned down the offer, ostensibly to take care of his own pressing affairs. (He planned one more expedition, which he intended to finance with his reward, but the schooner he had built in Canada sank in the Great Lakes.) As it was, the journey was left to James Anderson, a forty-three-year-old Company man whose chief claim to fame, in the eyes of his employers, was his cost-saving bookkeeping techniques. Second-in-command was forty-year-old James Green Stewart, a man who had played an important role in expanding the company's Yukon trade.

Right from the outset, however, the two-boat expedition was handicapped by poor planning and personality conflicts. Stewart had arranged for inferior bark canoes, which were no match for the turbulent waters of the Great Fish. And with no Inuit interpreters, they learned nothing from the aboriginal hunting parties they encountered on the Arctic coast. They did find, however, wood and metal strips stamped "Mr. Stanley" (of the *Erebus*), which further corroborated the Inuit story as told to Rae.

Anderson's report to the Admiralty and his subsequent letter to Lady Franklin in 1856 merely fortified her resolve to send one more ship to King William Island and to search the vicinity by sledge. She had hoped to convince the government to supply the ship and crew. But with John Barrow gone, and new blood running the Admiralty, it wanted none of it. As far as it was concerned, Franklin and his men had all starved to death somewhere in the Arctic, although it never dared say so publicly. It simply struck the names of the crew from its books, effective March 31, 1854.

It wasn't quite that simple, however. Having raised public expectations and made heroes of men who had searched for the Northwest Passage, the Admiralty found it difficult to convince the public that the search was now a waste of time. Certainly, there were opinions expressed, for example by the editors of *Blackwood's Edinburgh Magazine*, who thought it prudent to resist further financial commitment to the search. But they were no match in the public arena for the persuasive powers of Lady Franklin. Had not these men "solved the problem which was the object of their labors, or, in the beautiful words of Sir John Richardson, 'forged the last link of the North-West Passage with their lives?'" she asked. "A mission so sacred is worthy of a Government which had grudged and spared nothing for its heroic soldiers and sailors in other fields of warfare, and will surely be approved by our gracious Queen, who overlooks none of her loyal subjects suffering and dying for their country's honour."

Lady Franklin was essentially blackmailing the Admiralty with the same kind of rhetoric it had used to manipulate public opinion to its favor. By June 1856, so much public sympathy had been aroused by her that thirty-six of London's most distinguished men, including the venerable Sir Roderick Murchison, president of the Royal Geographic Society, were calling on the government to "satisfy the honour of the country, and clear up a mystery which has excited the sympathy of the civilized world." The government again refused, leaving Lady Franklin no choice but to put up her own money for the purchase of a small screw yacht called the *Fox*. On April 18, 1857, the command of the *Fox* was offered to McClintock.

With three Arctic expeditions behind him and more miles of sledging than anyone else in the navy, McClintock was in a perfect position to learn from the mistakes of the past. And so was his principal backer. Lady Franklin had pushed long and hard for the kind of search necessary to find her husband. And now that she was footing most of the bill, with her own money and that of private backers, no detail would be spared. At 177 tons (160 570 kg), the *Fox* was the kind of small, manoeuvrable vessel that Scoresby had advocated half a century earlier. Under McClintock's supervision, the ship was refitted completely to meet the Arctic challenge: the false keel was taken off, the sharp stem encased in iron, and the slender propeller replaced by a massive iron one. The crew would be small, but experienced—seventeen of the twenty-five having previously served in the Arctic search. Included among them was Carl Petersen, the remarkable Dane who had acted as interpreter and guide for Penny and Kane in previous expeditions. Christian, a Greenlandic Inuk, was hired to do the hunting and take care of the dogs. Both would be picked up in Greenland. The salted pork was still there, but augmented this time with 6682

*In 1857, by the light of lanterns, Leopold McClintock and his men bury crewman Robert Scott, who died from injuries sustained in a fall.*

pounds (3034 kg) of a North American Indian food called pemmican, made up of lean meat, pounded and mixed with melted fat.

Ironically, while McClintock had gone to great pains to ensure his ability to travel overland and to spend more than one season in the Arctic, he very nearly didn't make it to Lancaster Sound. Once again, the density of the Arctic ice proved to be a problem. After reaching, and then departing from, Greenland, the *Fox* spent 242 days struggling with the icepack at Melville Bukt, drifting south across Baffin Bay and Davis Strait with it for 1385 miles (2230 km) before finally breaking free. At Buchan Island, off the Greenland coast, the ship was nearly overturned when its bow struck a reef just as the tide was beginning to fall. At low water, the *Fox* inclined at a precarious thirty-five degrees. The water covered the starboard gunwale from the mainmast aft "and reached almost up to the hatchway [when] the slightest shake [might] have caused her to fall over upon her side [where] she would instantly have filled and sunk." Fortunately, the punishing ice floes stayed clear until the tide returned and righted the *Fox*. McClintock then sailed her into the North Water and reached the entrance to Lancaster Sound on July 14, 1858, 240 years to the day that Baffin and Bylot sailed "without hindrance" along the same coast and discovered Lancaster Sound.

At Pond Inlet on Baffin Island, an old woman remembered not only Parry over-wintering in Repulse Bay thirty-seven years earlier, but Inglefield's visit, and described the location of a wreck 45 miles (72 km) to the northwest. However, neither she nor other Inuit hunters encountered later on knew anything about the *Erebus* and *Terror*. McClintock was now certain about one thing. "Did other wrecks exist near at hand, our Pond's Bay [Inlet] friends would be much better supplied with wood. If the Esquimaux knew of anything within 300, 400, or even 500 miles, the Pond's Bay natives would at least have heard of them."

The only places left to search, then, were the unknown regions to the southwest, near King William Island. McClintock planned to proceed there by way of Peel Sound, after first depositing a marble tablet devoted to the memory of Franklin and his crew at Beechey Island. That accomplished, the *Fox* reached Peel Sound only to find the way blocked with ice. His situation now was desperate. There was only one chance left: retreat back through Barrow Strait and try to reach King William Island via Prince Regent Inlet and Bellot Strait.

But did Bellot Strait even exist? Both Bellot and Captain William Kennedy had thought they had seen a passage on their 1265-mile (2037-km) sledge journey in 1852 along the coast of Somerset and Boothia while searching for Franklin, but an outbreak of scurvy prevented them from confirming it. "Poor Bellot himself doubted it, and [William] Kennedy, his commander, could not positively assert that it did," McClintock thought to himself at the time. "And if there be a strait, is it free from ice?" McClintock had little choice but to try. (Anthropologist James Savelle and polar historian Clive Holland have recently analysed new and old evidence that suggests that John Ross missed a splendid opportunity to discover Bellot Strait and the Northwest Passage in 1832. They suggest that the humiliating pain he suffered ten years earlier, after having been turned back from Lancaster Sound because of the mythical Croker Mountains, combined with the distress associated with three years in the Arctic, undermined his confidence in recognizing and pursuing a potentially major geographic discovery.)

A long summer typically lasts until mid-August in Barrow Strait; McClintock and his crew saw the last of it on August 16 on their retreat eastward. With fog overtaking them, they were forced to drift with the ice towards Prince Leopold Island. Only weeks earlier, the imposing rock monolith had been swarming with hundreds of thousands of northern fulmars, black-legged kittiwakes, glaucous gulls, thick-billed murres, and black guillemots. Back then, they had shot in one day 1000 thick-billed murres and a handful of peregrine falcons, which Petersen described as "the best beef in the country." But now the birds were nearly all gone. And so were most of the beluga whales, which migrate in groups of up to 2000 to molt in the shallow, gravel-bottom bays along Somerset's coast.

It had begun to snow. In fact, it was snowing so hard by the time they got to Fury Beach, where Parry's ship had been hurled onto the gravel shores in 1824 under much the same conditions, that they were carried past it by the strong current before anyone was even aware of it. On August 21, they approached Brentford Bay, where the landscape changes dramatically from stark limestone gravel beaches to a rugged Precambrian upland. McClintock searched anxiously from the bow, then breathed a sigh of "intense relief" as he saw ice "streaming out of it." Bellot Strait—nearly 20 miles (32 km) long and barely a mile wide—really did exist!

McClintock wasted no time in preparing for the long winter. Once the crew had passed safely through Bellot Strait, they set up winter camp at Point Kennedy, then spent time adding to the food supply by hunting for caribou, seals, hares, polar bears, and wolves. As on other voyages, the hunting helped ease the boredom, for the *Fox* was too small a vessel to accommodate the theatre, newspaper publishing, and games that other larger expeditions had engaged in in the past. Besides, McClintock had other plans. In the dead of winter, using the light of the moon to guide them, he sent out three parties to set up the food and provision caches necessary for the long spring searches.

John Franklin's Land
Exploration and
Last Expedition (1845 – 47)

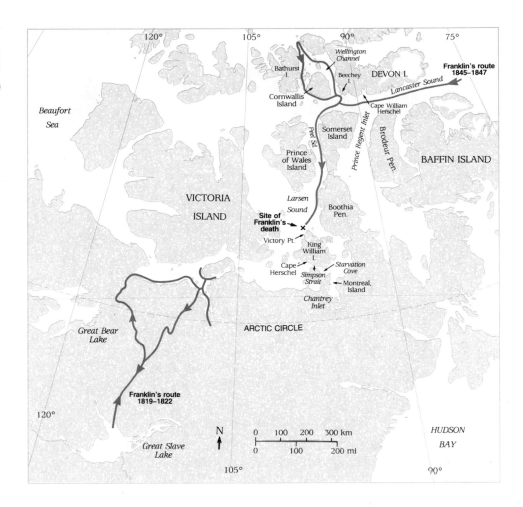

On one such preparatory expedition, down the Boothia coast, he met a group of Inuit, one of whom was wearing a naval button on his coat. He told McClintock that the button had come from some white men who starved on an island at the mouth of a river somewhere to the south. McClintock offered to buy whatever relics the Inuit could collect and was very quickly obliged. The next day, forty-five of their comrades arrived with gold chains, several buttons, and knives made of iron and wood from the wreck of a ship, which one of them said had sunk out in the sea to the west of King William Island. Although none of them had seen any white men, they related second-hand reports that the men aboard the ship had landed safely.

There was no question now in McClintock's mind that Rae's report was correct. But what of the other ship? Had it sunk? None of the Inuit seemed to know. McClintock was able to determine with some certainty that the men of the *Erebus* and *Terror* had at no time landed on Boothia Peninsula, as he searched its western shoreline carefully himself. If any trace of them was to be found, he concluded, it would be somewhere to the west, or farther south, towards the Great Fish River. There was an outside chance that they might have retreated to the northwest in the area of Prince of Wales Island in the hopes of joining up with some whalers.

On April 2, 1859 three search parties set out, equipped with a peculiar blend of North American know-how and British naval decorum. Using Inuit-fashioned dog teams, some of the men were wearing fur garments, others skin boots. The ship, however, hoisted the Royal Harwich Yacht flag in traditional fashion while each of the sledges was adorned with "gay silk banners";

McClintock's, he recalls, was a "very beautiful one," bearing the name of Lady Franklin in white letters and margined with white embroidery. Going native was one thing; British tradition was another!

While Captain Allen Young headed northwest, McClintock and his second-in-command, Lieutenant William Hobson, set off with two parties to the southwest with the idea of splitting up once they got to King William Island. On the eighteenth day, McClintock again encountered the Inuit group that he had met in February. There was now a young man with them who told of two ships that had been seen west of King William Island, one sunk in deep water, the other broken up on shore sometime during the autumn. In this ship on shore, the Inuit had found the body of a man, very tall and with exceptionally long teeth, sitting dead. During that same autumn, he said, the remainder of the crew departed for a "large river" to the south, hauling one or more boats with them. The following winter, their bones were found in that vicinity. McClintock now had a clear idea of what lay ahead of him. Hobson was sent to investigate the west coast of King William Island, while McClintock headed along the east coast to the mouth of the Great Fish River.

As pleasant as the Arctic may be in late April and May, traveling can still be hazardous. With the advent of twenty-four-hour daylight, the sun reflects off the white snow with excruciatingly painful brightness. To avoid the ravages of snow blindness, which feels similar to having sand in the eye, McClintock and his party restricted their traveling to the evenings, when the effect of the light is softened. It wasn't long before they encountered more Inuit families. From one group, McClintock purchased six pieces of silver plate bearing the crests or initials of Franklin, Francis Crozier, captain of the H.M.S. *Terror*, James Fairholme, lieutenant aboard the *Erebus*, and Alexander McDonald, the assistant surgeon. According to an old woman, she knew of the wreck, but little of it remained now. The white men, she added, had retreated to the Great River, but many of them "dropped by the way."

It must have seemed insane to McClintock, a man who knew all too well the remarkable physical strain associated with overland sledging, that Franklin and his men had retreated south with so many useless luxuries. Surely, if they were still healthy and searching for a means of escape, these would be the last sorts of objects to be weighed down with. And if they were in desperate shape? Even better reason to leave them behind. His arrival at Montreal Island a few days later did nothing to solve the mystery. There were no Inuit and barely a trace of the lost crew in the snow-covered region. All he found was a piece of preserved meat tin, two pieces of iron hoop, some scraps of copper, and an iron hook-bolt. The only thing to do now, McClintock decided, was to head back up the west coast of King William Island along the shores where the retreating crew must have marched.

As McClintock headed past Point Ogle, across Simpson Strait, he just missed Starvation Cove, where he probably would have found bodies at one of the Franklin party's last encampments. Within a day's march, however, he came upon the kind of evidence he was looking for—a human skeleton (later identified as that of officer Harry Peglar), perfectly bleached, lying face-first in the snow, with its limbs scattered about and gnawed away by small animals. McClintock searched more closely; there were a few scraps of clothing and a pocketbook. It was evident, McClintock believed, that the "poor man had selected the bare top ridge, as affording the least tiresome walking, and to have

*For many years, the European explorers failed to make use of Inuit innovations such as sun goggles used to protect the eyes from snow blindness.*

fallen upon his face in that position in which we found him.... It was a melancholy truth," he remarked, that the old Inuit woman whom he spoke with earlier had stated that "they fell down and died as they walked along."

Finally, with some first-hand evidence, McClintock thought he might soon have the answers concerning the missing men's fate. At Cape Herschel, he knew, Thomas Simpson had built a cairn twenty years earlier. There was no doubt in his mind that the Franklin crew had passed this way and deposited a record of their intended course of travel, which quite evidently included the discovery of the Northwest Passage. But all that remained there was a pile of rocks 4 feet (122 cm) high, which had evidently been pulled down and searched, probably by some inquisitive Inuit. Whatever secrets it once contained had disappeared. "Doubtless the natives, when they ascertained that famine and fatigue had caused many of the white men to fall down and die upon their fearful march...lost no time in following up their traces, examining every spot where they halted, every mark they put up, or stone displaced," McClintock wrote.

*One of a number of untitled paintings by Julius von Payer representing the final episode of John Franklin's expedition. The nightmarish scene illustrates how the British dismissed the Arctic as a barren, hostile place following the disappearance of Franklin and his crew.*

Would there then be any record of their fate and achievements? Another 12 miles (19 km) up the coast, McClintock found his answer in a small cairn built by Hobson's party six days earlier. Inside were two documents, written a year apart, that Hobson had found at a cairn at Victory Point on the northwest shore. The first from Lieutenant Graham Gore, a career officer who had narrowly escaped death while traveling with George Back in the *Terror*'s 1837 expedition, was dated May 28, 1847. It simply stated that the *Erebus* and *Terror* had wintered at Beechey Island in 1846–47, ascended Wellington Channel, and returned by the west side of Cornwallis Island. An "all well" at the end of the note indicated no problems.

The second, however, conveyed a more ominous development. Signed by ships' captains Francis Crozier and James Fitzjames, it was dated "April 25, 1848," and stated that "H.M. ships 'Terror' and 'Erebus' were deserted on the 22nd April, 5 leagues N.N.W. of this, having been beset since 12th September, 1846. The officers and crews, consisting of 105 souls, under the command of Captain F.R.M. Crozier, landed here in lat. 69 degrees 37′, 42′ N., long. 98 degrees 41′ W. Sir John Franklin died on the 11th June 1847: and the total loss by deaths in the expedition has been to this date 9 officers and 15 men."

These documents are the only first-hand records ever found describing what happened to the Franklin expedition after the whalers last saw them in Baffin Bay in 1845. But what a story their few lines tell. In 1847, Franklin and his men were only 90 miles (145 km) from the known sea and certain discovery of the Northwest Passage. They must have felt confident that the following spring would bring them to their glory. And then Franklin died. One of the ships sank, the other was hurled on shore by the moving ice. With only enough provisions to take them through July 1848, Crozier, the new commander, apparently decided to abandon the ship and head for the coastline to Back's Great Fish River. Had he hoped either to travel overland to Great Slave Lake or simply to find more game? With more than 100 people to feed and only shotguns with which to hunt, either would have been a hopeless task.

McClintock continued his search, reaching the north end of King William Island by the end of May. There he discovered a boat that Hobson had investigated earlier, 28 feet (854 cm) long, 7 feet (214 cm) wide, resting on a huge wooden sledge. McClintock estimated that it must have weighed a total of 1400 pounds (636 kg), an incredible weight to be hauled. Inside the boat, however, was something that "transfixed [him] with awe"; in the bow, was a skeleton of a slight young man that had been dismembered by animals. Beneath the after-thwart lay another skeleton in a better preserved state, wrapped in furs and cloths. What amazed McClintock even more were the number of objects scattered about. These included five watches, two double-barrelled shotguns (both loaded and cocked), and five or six small books spread out among "an amazing quantity of clothing." There were eight pairs of boots of various kinds, slippers, towels, silk handkerchiefs, soap, sponge, toothbrush, haircombs, twine, nails, saws, files, bristles, wax-ends, sail-makers' palms, powder, bullets, and a variety of other things that McClintock described as "dead weight, of little use, and very likely to break down the strength of the sledge-crews." The only food was some tea and about 40 pounds (18 kg) of chocolate—hardly enough to sustain anyone for any length of time.

In August 1984, Canadian anthropologist Owen Beattie and a team of scientists exhumed the body of John Torrington from his grave on Beechey

*Photograph of Franklin crew member John Torrington after his grave was unearthed in 1984. Torrington died on board the H.M.S. Terror on January 1, 1846 at the age of 20. Forensic anthropologist Owen Beattie and a team of scientists exhumed the body in an attempt to determine the cause of death.*

*The graves of John Torrington and other Franklin crew members on Beechey Island.*

Island. An autopsy was unable to ascertain the cause of death, but there was evidence of tuberculosis and anthracosis (blackened lungs), a condition brought on by the inhalation of pollutants such as coal dust and tobacco. As well, high levels of lead were also discovered in bone and hair samples, which likely originated from the soldering on the tinned meat cans. Beattie believes that lead poisoning may have contributed to the demise of the rest of the crew as it produces debilitating symptoms that can leave its victims disoriented.

McClintock himself believed that the surviving crew members knew exactly what they were doing right up to the last weeks or even days of their lives. One thing that seemed to convince him of this was the position of the boat. He was "astonished" to find it pointed directly to the northeast, aimed at the next point of land that he was also heading for. It was just 50 miles (81 km) from Victory Point and thus about 65 miles (105 km) from the position of the ship. Montreal Island was 150 miles (242 km) behind. McClintock convincingly argues that the men were returning to the ship from Montreal Island and found that they could save themselves 40 miles (64 km) by crossing over 10 or 12 miles (16 or 19 km) of low land. Then, as exhaustion overtook them, they realized that they had "greatly overrated their strength" and chose to leave the boat behind. Either they couldn't drag it any farther or there was no sense doing so because they planned to return to it for another attempt south the following spring. The two men that stayed with it, he assumed, probably couldn't keep pace, so they were left with some provisions until the others could return from the ship with fresh supplies. However, given the fact that no more bodies were found, they obviously did not return.

Finding neither of the ships, and none of the graves, McClintock returned to Bellot Strait after seventy-eight days of sledging to find Hobson sick with scurvy and the ship's steward dead. He had apparently succumbed as a result of his disdain for fresh game and pemmican, salted pork being his principal source of protein. Captain Young had returned prematurely from his journey after a brief illness, then set out again against the doctor's orders. He got back to the *Fox* on June 28, with no news of Franklin but the mapping of Prince of Wales Island completed.

Back home the following September, McClintock conveyed the details of his sad findings to Lady Franklin and the British public. Wisely, he avoided being as blunt as Rae had been before him. As pathetic and avoidable as the Franklin crew's demise was, McClintock chose to emphasize the positive. "Virtual completion of the North-West Passage" had been attained by Franklin and his men, he declared. Although Franklin was probably not there when Gore or someone else first spotted Queen Maud Gulf to the west, it was Franklin and Richardson who had discovered and mapped a great part of it up until then.

It was just the kind of brave, noble ending that the public wanted to hear. Newspapers lauded Franklin as an international hero. "Our age is the age of chivalry," said *The New York Times*; and Franklin was "a man of this generation." Indeed, as Richardson had said from the outset of the search, everyone now truly believed that the men of the *Erebus* and *Terror* had "forged the last link of the North-West Passage with their lives." Great Britain, with the rest of the world applauding her, had finally achieved what so many other countries had aspired to for centuries. The route through the Northwest Passage finally belonged to Britain, alone.

Forgotten in the rejoicing, of course, were the North American Indian and Inuit guides. Matonabbee, Akaitcho, Augustus, Maufelly, Ouligbuck, Christian, and all of the other native explorers who had guided, fed, clothed, and sometimes nursed so many Northwest Passage explorers were simply reduced to footnotes in the published diaries of the journeys. All the glory was reserved for the white man, though he rarely deserved it. Still, there was at least one touching farewell that indicated that the contributions of the native people were not entirely forgotten. When Rae headed home in 1854 from his last expedition, he presented William Ouligbuck with a "very handsomely mounted hunting knife." It had been put in his care by Sir George Back as a memento of the 1825–27 overland journey that William's father had made with Back and Franklin. The elder Ouligbuck, however, could not be there to receive it. He had died in the autumn of 1852.

McClintock's voyage did little to prevent others from searching for further clues to the disappearance of the Franklin expedition. Indeed, that search continues to this very day. But two expeditions, which began soon after McClintock's return to England, are significant in that they reinforced the importance of "going native" and the basic fallacy behind the Victorian view of the sublime Arctic. The first was a series of searches conducted by American newspaper entrepreneur Charles Francis Hall between 1860 and 1869; the second, headed by Frederick Schwatka between 1878 and 1880, was sponsored by the American Geographical Society.

Hall's first two ventures northward were anything but successful in finding clues about Franklin, which was not surprising given the fact that he had no experience in navigation, no survival skills, and no significant financial backing. On the first voyage in 1860, he simply hitched a ride aboard a whaling vessel and disembarked on the shores of what was then still regarded as Frobisher Strait. As far-fetched as his plan was to make his way to King William Island, it was effectively killed when a storm wrecked two of the whaling vessels that had brought him to Frobisher Strait as well as the small boat he had hoped to use for his own searches. His second expedition, from 1864 to 1869, leaving from the northwest shore of Hudson Bay, did not fare any better. After being dropped off in the wrong place, he experienced further obstacles to progress in the form of misunderstandings with Inuit guides, harsh weather, and his own unstable temperament. In fact, it wasn't until 1869 that Hall finally made it to King William Island. There he found only a few relics and some bones of Franklin's crew.

Success, however, didn't entirely elude Hall on his first two expeditions, thanks to a single magical encounter on his first journey to Frobisher Strait, which occurred while he was in his cabin on the *George Henry*, the only whaling vessel to survive the storm. While Hall was working intently at his desk, a "soft, sweet, voice," bidding him "Good morning, sir," drew his attention. Astonished that a lady of refinement had somehow come so far north, he turned round, certain that he was dreaming. But there, indeed, was a feminine shadow standing in a flood of light streaming in from the skylight, wearing "crinoline, heavy flounces, an attenuated toga, and an immensely expanded 'kiss-me-quick' bonnet." The woman, who emerged from the shadows extending an ungloved hand, was no lady from New York or London, but a "lady Esquimaux," simple, gentle and extremely graceful.

Her name was Tookoolito, and she and her husband, Ebierbing, had been taken to England years earlier by a British whaling vessel. "Eskimo Joe" and "Hannah," as the white men called them, had even dined with Prince Albert and met Queen Victoria herself. Ebierbing confessed that he liked her very much and found her "quite pretty."

It was the beginning of a long and loyal friendship that was to serve Hall well in his quest for discovery, and Ebierbing and Tookoolito in their own passion for new adventures. On Baffin Island, the couple became Hall's tutors in the ways of Inuit survival, acquainting him with their food, their igloo homes, and their methods of hunting. They also acted as his interpreters. The lessons proved that even a novice in the art of Arctic exploration could learn to adapt. It wasn't long before Hall was comfortable enough to venture off alone on several overland expeditions with the Inuit, as Hearne had done with the Indians nearly a century before him. But as much as he exulted in his own survival skills, Hall, like Hearne, was very much a hostage to the natives' whims. Although he was a big and brazen individual, his Inuit guides took him where he wanted to go only if it suited them. And many times during their overland treks, it did not.

Although Hall learned little about the fate of the Franklin crew on these overland treks of his, he did make at least two important discoveries on Baffin Island. One was that Frobisher Strait was indeed a bay. (The so-called Zeno map was still a great source of confusion.) Then, from stories told to him by Ebierbing's grandmother—of two ships, then three, then many more arriving in successive seasons—he was able to find a number of relics—including coal, flint-stone, tile, glass, pottery, and the ruins of a stone house and mining excavation on and around Kodlunarn Island. The discovery was the first conclusive proof that Martin Frobisher had indeed visited this part of the

*American explorer Charles Francis Hall with Tookoolito and Ebierbing. Hall's farfetched hopes of solving the Franklin mystery were at least made credible with the aid and guidance of the Baffin Island couple.*

world. From other Inuit legends, Hall also learned that the five men of Frobisher's first expedition who had been left behind had attempted to build a boat out of the scraps discarded by the expedition. However, the ice never gave them a chance to launch it, and it wasn't long before they died of starvation.

Hall returned from his second expedition without anything important to contribute to the Franklin mystery, other than a rumor that some Inuit children had been given some papers from the expedition to play with. But in the public's hunger for stories of the Arctic and adventure, he became a celebrity nonetheless. Individuals as important as President Ulysses S. Grant came to hear him lecture, while Lady Jane Franklin, who initially doubted the wisdom of what he had set out to do, widely praised his efforts. With so much to recommend him, he had no trouble raising enough funds to acquire a ship and a scientific crew (headed by a German, Dr. Emil Bessels) for an expedition in search of the north geographic pole. This search for the Pole was among the first of many more to follow.

It was on this journey that Hall's luck finally ran out. Two weeks after his *Polaris* departed from New London, Connecticut, in July 1871, he took seriously ill, refused all medication from Bessels, and complained loudly that the German was trying to poison him. He soon died of what Bessels later diagnosed as a stroke. A board of inquiry accepted his medical report, and that cause of death remained official until 1968, when Chauncey Loomis exhumed his body and sent samples of it for examination to the Centre for Forensic Medicine in Toronto. The centre's report indicated that Hall had been fed a toxic amount of arsenic during the last two weeks of his life.

The death of Hall left Eibierbing and Tookolito alone in the United States, believing that they would never go north again. Eibierbing, however, did go back twice more, once with Allen Young in 1876, on board the *Pandora*, in an unsuccessful attempt to navigate through the Northwest Passage, and again in 1878 with U.S. Cavalry officer Frederick Schwatka, after returning to the United States to find his beloved Tookolito had died. The Schwatka expedition had evolved out of reports from American whaling captain Thomas Barry who claimed to have been given a silver spoon bearing the crest of Franklin during a previous trip to Repulse Bay. He also reported overhearing some Inuit hunters talking about documents relating to the expedition that lay in a cairn on an island in the Gulf of Boothia. Barry had conveyed this story to James Gordon Bennett of the *New York Herald*, whose interests in the Arctic had been whetted by his involvement with the *Pandora* expedition. It was time, he felt, for another search for Franklin. He immediately set the wheels in motion and got the American Geographical Society involved.

Like Rae's expeditions, Schwatka's was small, light, and maneuverable and was carried out with tireless determination. But any hopes of attaining its goals were killed once the expedition reached Hudson Bay. There, a whaling captain convinced Schwatka's party that Barry's claim of overhearing the Inuit talking about books and documents from the Franklin expedition was "supremely ridiculous." Only two non-native people in the world could understand exactly what they were saying, he insisted, and Barry was certainly not one of them. Furthermore, he said, he himself had been given three spoons identical to the one described by Barry. One of them just happened to be missing. It was a rude welcome for a group of men who had such high hopes of finding the missing clues to what had happened to the Franklin expedition.

*An iceberg, probably calved from a glacier in Greenland, drifts through Lancaster Sound.*

As William Gilder, the *New York Herald* journalist who was a part of the expedition, described it afterwards, the party had quite evidently "come on a fool's errand."

One has to admire Schwatka's response to this depressing bit of news. Instead of giving up and returning home, as he would have been justified in doing, he decided to press on to King William Island on the outside chance that he might uncover something. The sledge journey that ensued was one of the greatest on record. By throwing in their lot completely with the Inuit and their ways, the overland party, which occasionally broke up into two groups, was able to cover 3230 miles (5200 km) in less than a year. The weather did not always co-operate—the temperatures often dipped to below −50°F (−46°C)—but no one suffered any serious injury or debilitating health. The ways of the natives, which had been shunned for so long by so many Northwest Passage explorers, had more than proved their worth on this journey.

At King William Island, Schwatka did, in fact, discover bones and partial skeletons of the Franklin crew. These, his party gave a proper burial. They also found a number of relics, including part of a boat, that they carried back home. More importantly, however, Schwatka was able to confirm from the Inuit of the area a story that had been relayed earlier to Hall—that documents pertaining to the Franklin expedition had indeed been found by the natives, but were given to the children to play with. Hence, there was now virtually no chance of ever finding out what exactly had happened to the *Erebus* and *Terror*. Those secrets, in all likelihood, forever belong to the wind, the rain, and the elements.

# A CHANGING WORLD

A young Inuk dressed in southern clothing zooms down a slide in Cambridge Bay on Victoria Island.

A high school student from Iqaluit on Baffin Island.

*A kayak expedition in Pond Inlet. Tourism is a growing industry in the Arctic.*

*The Polaris lead-zinc mine, owned by Cominco, is the most northerly metal mine in the world. This underground mine is located on Little Cornwallis Island north of Barrow Strait.*

*Igloo-shaped houses in Nanasivik, a lead-zinc mining community on northern Baffin Island.*

"I had expected to find these people living in quite a primitive state, and in this respect, was disappointed beyond measure. What we did find was the worst kind of tinpot store and canned provision culture…. And when a powerful gramophone struck up, and Caruso's mighty voice rang out from Igjugarjuk's tent, I felt we had missed our market, as far as the study of these people were concerned. We were about a hundred years too late."
—KNUD RASMUSSEN, FIFTH THULE EXPEDITION, 1922

# 6.
# SCIENCE
# AND
# SOVEREIGNTY

---

I t fell upon the Royal Canadian Mounted Police between 1953 and 1956 to transport seventy-four Inuit from Inoucdjouac in northern Quebec to an airfield weather station at Resolute Bay and to the RCMP outpost at Craig Harbour in the High Arctic. (The original plan was to take some of the Inuit to Melville Island, but ice conditions enabled the boat carrying them to get only as far as Cornwallis Island. The Craig Harbour group eventually settled at Grise Fiord at the south end of Ellesmere Island.) The Canadian government's idea, at least as it was presented to the Inuit at the time, was to provide them with better hunting opportunities, for the scarcity of caribou in northern Quebec had caused considerable hunger, and at times, starvation. A handful of Baffin Islanders would go with them to be their guides and teachers in the new land.

Some shock was expressed decades later when the Canadian public became aware of this uprooting. It was, however, by no means a novel idea. In expanding its commercial operations from the boreal forest, the Hudson's Bay Company had frequently used its vessels to transport Inuit families to new Arctic outposts. It had done so in 1934 when nine families from Pond Inlet, Cape Dorset, and Pangnirtung were taken to the largely uninhabited environs of Dundas Harbour, where the company intended to establish a new trading post. The Inuit were brought along to take in a harvest of furs and sealskins for the post. It was essentially a mutually beneficial arrangement. While the Hudson's Bay Company was getting the people it needed to trade with in the area, those Inuit—already well-acquainted with a nomadic existence—were

*Children race through the community of Pangnirtung on Cumberland Sound.*

being provided with better access to animals and to the supplies the company's trading facility would offer.

The government's plan to move the Inoucdjouac Inuit to Resolute Bay and to Craig Harbour, on the other hand, entailed something quite different. For one thing, the RCMP hadn't told them that they weren't all destined to go to the same place. For another, the new settlements would be markedly different to what they had been accustomed. In the High Arctic, the Inoucdjouac would have to adapt to about four months of total darkness and, in the case of Resolute on Cornwallis Island, to a stark landscape that does not sustain any appreciable population of large land mammals.

In the long run, the people of Resolute and Grise Fiord persevered despite the inevitable hardships. For some, there was continued resentment at the loss of family and friends, the passing away of those who succumbed to the stress of a new life, and the refusal of the Canadian government, at least until 1988, to honor a commitment to send back home to northern Quebec anyone who, after two years, wasn't content with the new settlement. However, none of the ill-will quite matched the anger that was expressed when a number of the Inoucdjouac inadvertently discovered that the real reason for their unusual migration lay in Canada's desire to assert sovereignty over the Northwest Passage and the Canadian Arctic Archipelago. Canada's secret aim from the beginning was to prove to the rest of the world that it had a so-called "human stake" in the area, which, in turn, would justify its legal claim to the land and waters of the Arctic Archipelago.

This desperate drive to assert sovereignty over the High Arctic was, in many ways, a catch-up affair for Canada. Not until November 4, 1879, a little more than twelve years after Canada had become a nation, did Britain reluctantly transfer "all British Territories and Possessions in North America, not already included within the Dominion of Canada, and all Islands adjacent to any such Territories and Possessions." However, that order, which took effect in October 1880, was so vaguely worded that Canada's jurisdiction was left in considerable doubt until October 1895 when Canada passed an order-in-council clarifying its intentions. By that time, international interest in the Arctic had reached the point where many countries—Great Britain, the United States, Germany, Denmark, and Norway—were not entirely sympathetic to the young nation's newfound aspirations.

With the new international interest in the Arctic that unfolded in the era after Franklin, there was a corresponding development in the progress of science. As American historian Daniel J. Boorstin put it, "modern times brought with them new instruments of publicity." Among them were a more efficient printing press and broader-based scientific societies. The net effect was to make it easier for intellectuals to promote and exchange ideas. Unfortunately for Canada, which lacked a strong scientific tradition, these were developments from which it could not immediately benefit.

One of the first people in the post-Franklin period to promote the idea of putting science on the front burner of future Arctic explorations was an Austrian naval officer, Lieutenant Karl Weyprecht. In a speech to the German Natural Philosophers and Physicians conference at Graz, Austria, in 1875, he argued that the sometimes frivolous and greedy search for discovery of the Northwest and Northeast passages had undermined important scientific research that would have benefited human understanding of the laws of

*The old RCMP post at Pierce Point on the northwest side of Darnley Bay, near the Inuit village of Paulatuk.*

nature. And so he proposed a plan for international scientific co-operation in the polar region. Four years later, a polar conference in Hamburg adopted his recommendations, and, by 1881, the year Weyprecht died at the young age of forty-three, there was enough interest for the establishment of twelve research stations in the Arctic and another three in the Antarctic. More than 700 men and eleven countries participated in this, the first International Polar Year. Canada, however, was not one of them, although it did help Great Britain establish an observatory at Fort Rae in the Northwest Territories.

This new emphasis on science by no means subverted the impetus behind exploration for exploration's sake. Instead, it established yet another justification for it, which was necessary, given the void that had been created with the Franklin tragedy. At the forefront of this new *raison d'être*, however, was a view of the world that no longer trusted in the harmony between man and nature or perceived the Arctic world through the ill-fitting aesthetics of the Sublime and the Picturesque. Rather, it looked towards the Arctic with the kind of perceptual framework that Charles Darwin had adopted while exploring the Galàpagos Islands during the middle part of the nineteenth century. Just as Darwin ultimately saw the strange plants and animals that he encountered as natural adaptations to a unique environment, so too did the new generation of Arctic explorer/scientists as they made their way through the lands and waters of the Northwest Passage. As a result, distinctive Arctic geological formations, such as pingos, polygons, and glacial flutings, eventually came to be seen for what qualities they possessed, not what they lacked.

By far, the most successful of the new Arctic explorers were the Scandinavians. Influenced by the Darwinian view of the world and inspired by the successful Northeast Passage voyage of Finnish scientist Adolf Erik Nordenskiold in 1878–79, they developed and improved on a number of technologies and ideas that exploited the uniqueness of the Arctic landscape to their advantage. Granted, Salomon Andrée's use of a giant balloon to fly over the impenetrable ice around the North Pole in 1897 was ill-conceived and ended disastrously. But Fridtjof Nansen's employment of skis and sledges to cross the Greenland icecap in 1888, his adaptation of Inuit clothing designs, his reliance on fresh game, and his use of Eskimo dogs dramatically improved the art of Arctic travel.

Nansen's most important contribution, however, arose from his brilliant idea to exploit the drift of the Arctic pack ice. This drift is propelled by an Arctic current that moves in a clockwise direction, from Siberia to Greenland, and was seen by Nansen as the reason why parts of the wreck of the *Jeannette*, a ship used by American explorer George De Long to reach the mythical open polar sea by way of the Bering Sea in 1879 – 81, were discovered years later off the coast of Greenland. Nansen saw the drift as a means of enabling him to reach the North Pole by sailing with the ice rather than against it. He was astute enough, however, to recognize that any vessel used for that purpose would have to be modified in a manner that would enable it to exploit the drift without suffering its crushing power. With this in mind, his colleague Otto Sverdrup worked with naval architect Colin Archer to build the *Fram*. It was a remarkable vessel, designed to be small and strong so that it could maneuver through the broken ice and narrow leads, yet large enough to carry a supply of coal, basic food provisions, and ten or twelve men for a period of five years. "The main point in this vessel is that it be built on such principles as to enable it to withstand the pressure of the ice," Nansen emphasized. "The sides must slope sufficiently to prevent the ice, when it presses together, from getting firm hold of the hull.... Instead of nipping the ship, the ice must raise it up out of the water." Although Nansen's attempt with Sverdrup to reach the North Pole with the *Fram* between 1893 and 1896 ultimately failed, he proved to his critics that the pack ice no longer had to be regarded as a barrier for ocean-going vessels, as it had been in the earlier part of the century.

Combining new technology with the traditional ways of the Inuit, the Scandinavians embarked on a series of sea and overland explorations in the post-Franklin era that took them across the Greenland icecap and into the unexplored regions of Canada's Arctic Archipelago. Ironically, Roald Amundsen, the most famous of them, attributes his early desire for adventure to Franklin's expeditions, as ill-conceived as they were. The "fervid fascination" with which he read Franklin's narratives, Amundsen confessed at a later point in his career, "shaped the whole course of my life," including his goal to be the first man to navigate through the elusive Northwest Passage.

There can, however, be no mistake about where Amundsen had learned his most valuable lessons, for his exploits followed closely in the footsteps of Nordenskiold, Nansen, and Sverdrup, rather than those of Franklin. To this tradition, Amundsen contributed a number of his own ideas. One of the most practical was the notion that many earlier polar explorations had failed because the commanders of the expeditions had not always been ships' captains. And so, in having to rely on the skippers that came along, the expeditions tended to have not one leader but two. This situation often resulted in the development of two hostile factions, Amundsen reasoned, with the commander and the scientific crew on one side, and the captain and ship's crew on the other. Amundsen vowed that he would never lead an expedition until he qualified as a ship captain, and he held himself to it.

In the United States, where discovery of the North Pole had become a national obsession in the late nineteenth and early twentieth centuries, prospective explorers could turn to the government, to private foundations, and to a host of wealthy entrepreneurs like James Gordon Bennett, owner of the *New*

*Fram Fiord, on southern Ellesmere Island, was named for Fridtjof Nansen's vessel.*

*York Herald*, for financial support. For a young man like Amundsen, looking to become the first to navigate the Northwest Passage in 1900, the funding task was a more formidable one. With the Franklin disaster, the allure of the Northwest Passage was no longer as strong as it once had been. Furthermore, the navigation of it had come to be considered too risky. Amundsen's strategy, consequently, was to promote the expedition as a scientific one. However, he knew that even this wouldn't be sufficient unless influential individuals like Nansen could be won over. "I knew that a word of encouragement from him would be priceless to me in enlisting aid in my enterprise," he said. "On the other hand, a word of disparagement from him would be fatal." Nansen generously gave Amundsen his approval, but the director of the British Observatory at Kew turned him down, while the director of the Meteorological Observatory at Oslo could only offer him a letter of introduction. Low on funds, but still hopeful, Amundsen finally decided to travel to Hamburg where he would try to arrange an interview with George von Neumayer, one of the world's leading scientific authorities on the Arctic and Antarctic. To his surprise, he was granted an audience. The great scientist was at first unimpressed with the young Norwegian's announcement that he wanted to be the first "to conquer the Northwest Passage." But when Amundsen added that he also wanted to establish the true location of the north magnetic pole, he told him, "If you do that, you will become the benefactor of mankind for ages to come. That is the great adventure."

With the support of both Nansen and von Neumayer secured, Amundsen managed to raise sufficient funds to put down a payment towards the purchase of a small fishing smack, which he named the *Gjoa*. At 47 tons (42.6 tonnes), with a 13-horsepower motor, the herring-cutter was, as Amundsen liked to point out, the same age as he was—thirty years old. He then spent the next few months in the North Atlantic, making oceanographic observations and turning the data over to Nansen in appreciation for all that the old explorer had done for him. But then, on the morning of June 16, 1903, the unthinkable happened. One of his most important creditors unexpectedly demanded full payment of debts in twenty-four hours or the boat would be seized and charges of fraud laid in the courts. With no money to pay him, Amundsen was thrown into a panic. Faced with the distinct possibility of never again having a chance like this one, he called upon his six expedition mates and explained the crisis to them. With everyone in full agreement, he and the others finished loading up what they could that same day and sailed quietly out of Christiania Harbor at midnight "in the perfect deluge of rain. When the dawn arose on our truculent creditor," Amundsen remarked later, "we were safely out on the open main, seven as light-hearted pirates as ever flew the black flag."

Clements Markham, the British historian and Arctic explorer, characterized the three-year voyage of the *Gjoa* as one of "extraordinary pluck and endurance and, it must be added, of scarcely less extraordinary good fortune." Amundsen sailed from Godhavn to the shores of North America without encountering the ice that had stalled McClintock's voyage for nearly a year in 1857. After paying his respects at the graves of the three Franklin crew members and that of Thomas Morgan of the *Investigator* on Beechey Island, he headed south into Peel Sound and passed without difficulties the point where Allen Young had been forced to retreat in 1875. But that's about as far as his luck carried him. After the ship nearly ran aground in Peel Sound, its engine room caught fire. A four-day gale soon followed and nearly blew the *Gjoa* ashore on the Boothia Peninsula. While desperately trying to find a place to shelter, Amundsen finally came upon what he later described as the "most beautiful little landlocked bay that the heart of a sailor could desire."

It was here, on King William Island where most of the Franklin crew members had perished, that Amundsen and his small party survived nicely for two winters, exploiting the "fat of the land," while they painstakingly conducted magnetic observations and studied the ways and habits of the Inuit. (It took twenty years of calculations to digest the entire meaning of the data of his magnetic observations.) Then, on August 13, 1905, they finally set sail through Simpson Strait, hoping to complete the Northwest Passage that same year. Four days after departure, the *Gjoa* passed the last unnavigated point at Cambridge Bay. Over the course of the next three weeks—"the longest three weeks of my life," Amundsen confessed—the tiny herring-cutter crept along slowly, winding its way through "the shallowness of these torturous channels." Amundsen was so unnerved by it all that he could not eat any food. Finally, after being out of contact with the non-native world for so long, he spotted a whaling ship from the Bering Strait side of the passage. Amundsen knew then that the worst was behind him and that his successful navigation of the passage would soon be a certainty.

Amundsen's ultimate triumph, however, had to be delayed for a year. A few days after spotting the whaler, the *Gjoa* ran into heavy pack ice, which it could not push through. The crew was thus forced to over-winter for a third year, this time at King Point on the north Yukon coast. While the crew settled down for

*The Gjoa's first meeting with whalers after completing the Northwest Passage.*

yet another season of magnetic observations, the restless Amundsen made an overland dash with a whaling captain whose ship had also been trapped in the ice. At Eagle, Alaska, some 500 miles (805 km) away, Amundsen sent news of his impending accomplishment to the outside world. It would be another season before he would sail the plucky herring-cutter into San Francisco Bay.

While Amundsen was proceeding on the last leg of his historic journey through the Northwest Passage, Canada was waking up to the fact that it was losing its hold on its northern frontier. Amundsen's voyage was the least troublesome for the government of Prime Minister Wilfrid Laurier, however. Of more concern were the sledge journeys conducted by Otto Sverdrup. Between 1898 and 1902, the Norwegian explorer conducted surveys of West Ellesmere, Axel Heiberg, Amund Ringnes, Ellef Ringnes, King Christian, Cornwall, and Graham islands. What's more, he claimed them for Norway. Initially complacent, the Laurier government stood up and took notice in 1905 when W.F. King, Canada's senior scientist and chief astronomer, confidentially advised the government that the country's claim over the Northwest Passage and Arctic Archipelago was not only "imperfect" but lacking international force. "Canada's title to the northern islands derived from Great Britain's," King pointed out. "Great Britain's title rests upon acts of discovery and possession. These acts were never, prior to the transfer to Canada, ratified by State authority, or confirmed by exercise of jurisdiction."

Two years earlier, an international tribunal of six jurists (three from the United States and three from Great Britain) had decided in favor of the Americans in a boundary dispute over the Yukon/Alaska frontier. In light of the apparent strong claim by Canada, many nationalists concluded that the British diplomats acting on behalf of the young nation made extraordinary compromises to promote their own relationship with the United States. As a result, the Laurier government was called upon to take diplomatic matters into its own hands rather than allow Canadian interests to be negotiated by a third party in London. If it didn't, the critics argued, the United States' insatiable desire to "possess the whole North American continent" would never be curbed.

In 1905, two new provinces, Alberta and Saskatchewan, were carved out of the Northwest Territories. The idea, in part, was to focus greater attention on the administration of the North and the activities of foreigners. But the logistics of monitoring foreign activities in the Arctic had already proved to be a daunting, if not impossible task, given the size of the area, the level of foreign activity, and the absence of scientific expertise and resources in Canada to do anything about it. By the turn of the century, American and British whalers were exploiting the waters of Davis Strait, Hudson Bay, and the Beaufort Sea in such large numbers that they threatened both the whale populations and the well-being of the Inuit. In the western Arctic alone, where whalers distributed liquor and taught the Inuit how to make it, alcoholism and its related problems had transformed the area into what anthropologist Diamond Jenness describes as a "hive of debauchery: drunkenness and immorality prevailed everywhere, strife and murder became everyday events, and disease previously unknown to the Eskimos began to sweep away old and young like flies," he said. "Syphilis took root among them, increasing the death rate, especially of infants, and causing apparent widespread infertility."

Faced with both a serious threat to the Inuit and to its sovereignty over the Arctic, the Laurier government responded by establishing a network of police

*A whaler stacking whalebone to dry on board ship, 1912.*

NATIONAL ARCHIVES OF CANADA/C-23655

forces and customs stations in the North. The first two were set up in 1903, at Herschel Island just north of the Yukon coast by Francis Joseph Fitzgerald and F.D. Sutherland, and at Cape Fullerton in Hudson Bay by J.D. Moodie. Moodie undertook this task midway through a patrol of Hudson Bay and the High Arctic in 1903–04 on the CGS *Neptune* with Albert Low of the Geological Survey of Canada. The two-year voyage was undertaken not only to monitor the whalers, but also to collect customs duties and to plant the Canadian flag over areas whose status might have remained in doubt. Low's conclusion "that the great waste of life in the killing of [whales and walrus], and the comparative small value to civilization" included a recommendation that Canada ban the killing, except in the case of the Inuit hunters.

In 1904 the Canadian government also purchased the 650-ton (590-tonne) *Gauss*, a sturdy, three-year-old sailing ship with an auxiliary steam engine, which had just returned from a two-year Antarctic expedition. The ship was renamed CGS *Arctic*, and then assigned to make eight voyages north, seven of them under the command of Joseph-Elzéar Bernier. A native of the small town of L'Islet in Quebec, Bernier was, like Amundsen, enthralled at a young age by the tales of British Arctic adventures. As early as 1898, he had stated for the record that he wanted to be the first Canadian to sail through the Northwest Passage and to stand at the north geographic pole. The sovereignty controversy in Canada very nearly got him his wish. Between 1906 and 1913, he discovered no new lands, but on one occasion, in 1909, he did pass halfway through the passage and was within range of completing it from Melville Island. However, he turned back because he did not have authorization to proceed. It must have been a terrible heartache for him, for when he was given the go-ahead the next year on the third and final series of prewar voyages, his route was blocked by the pack in McClure Strait, just as it had blocked the way of the *Investigator* heading in the opposite direction in 1851.

These low-key but noteworthy contributions to Canada's claim over the Northwest Passage and Arctic islands by Bernier, the Geological Survey of Canada, and the RCMP were largely eclipsed by the more flamboyant and controversial exploits of the Canadian-born American Vilhjalmur Stefansson. Stefansson was perhaps the most intriguing of the early twentieth-century explorers, not only for what he accomplished but for the manner in which he did it. Driven by the same kind of blind ambition that motivated McClure, he could be as thorny, contrary, and correct as a Richard King, yet he was blessed with the physical tenacity of a John Rae or an Otto Sverdrup. The Scandinavian explorers were merely his equals. As Stefansson himself would often suggest, he seemed, as an Icelander born in Canada, to have been destined to follow in the footsteps of his Viking ancestors and complete the discoveries that they had initiated nearly a thousand years earlier.

In reality, Stefansson stumbled into the world of Arctic exploration by chance. His first expedition to the Beaufort Sea in 1906–07, under the leadership of Danish naval adventurer Ejnar Mikkelsen and American geologist Ernest de Koven Leffingwell, came about because one of the backers demanded that a qualified ethnologist accompany the expedition. The two leaders looked to Harvard University, and Stefansson, as spotty as his scholastic record was at the time, got the recommendation, thanks to a professor who was intrigued by his Icelandic background and his study of Icelanders' diet. The expedition, which had hoped to find new lands in the Beaufort Sea, was largely a failure. Still, Stefansson returned from it confident in the notion, which he would come to repeat time and time again, that the secret to Arctic travel was to adapt to the ways of the Inuit.

Stefansson was also able to argue with confidence that Arctic exploration and polar research could be conducted safely, efficiently, and at one-tenth the cost of previous undertakings. It was by no means a novel idea, as Rae, Schwatka, and others had proved, but Stefansson refined the approach by emphasizing greater reliance on hunting fresh game and using snow houses in place of European food and heavy tents. More importantly, he made it sound like his own idea, and emerged, in the eyes of the uneducated public, a genius.

Stefansson's uncanny ability to promote himself through the popular press eventually secured him the support of the American Museum of Natural History for a second Arctic expedition in 1908. With a little more maneuvering by Stefansson, the Geological Survey of Canada became involved as well, if only because its directors were interested in gaining a little more prestige for Canadian science. Led jointly with Rudolph Anderson, a scientist with the

*Raising the Canadian flag at Canada Point on Bylot Island, August 21, 1906. Unfortunately, Captain Joseph-E. Bernier never realized his life-long dream of sailing through the Northwest Passage.*

NATIONAL ARCHIVES OF CANADA/PA-139394

Canadian government who had no Arctic experience, the expedition had only vague scientific plans, but they included Stefansson's special desire to track down an Inuit tribe on Victoria Island. This tribe was rumored to have some of the physical attributes of Caucasians, and Stefansson deduced that these "Blond Eskimos," who had no contact with the outside world up until then, may have been descendants of the original settlers of Greenland. The theory, of course, was pure conjecture on Stefansson's part, and there was little evidence to back it up; however, the publicity it generated was considerable. Fortunately for Stefansson, this attention came at a time when the Canadian government was feeling the heat of public opinion over Senator Paul Poirier's "sector theory" declaration in 1907. Poirier had warned that if Canada did not formally assert its sovereignty over the Arctic, it would have to forfeit it. Consequently, he urged that the Arctic be carved up like a pie, with the North Pole at the center, and divided among Norway, Sweden, the United States, Canada, and Russia. The declaration was not taken seriously initially, but with American institutions such as the American Museum of Natural History and the National Geographic Society sponsoring expeditions in the Arctic as if it were theirs, the Canadian government finally decided to sponsor a third expedition by Stefansson.

The Canadian Arctic expedition of 1913–18 was devoted to geographic discovery in the western Arctic regions and to the study of the Inuit. In this sense, it was an unqualified success. The northern division headed by Stefansson, with the help of his Inuit guide, Natkusiak, discovered and raised the Canadian flag on Brock, Borden, Meighen, and Lougheed islands (Stefansson's critics called them the "Tory archipelago" because they were named after conservative politicians in Canada) and virtually completed the mapping of the Arctic Archipelago. The southern division under Anderson, in the meantime, produced in a detailed scientific survey of the Coronation Gulf region and a landmark study of the Copper Inuit by anthropologist Diamond Jenness.

Nevertheless, it was near the outset of the expedition that the fate of Stefansson and of Canada's future Arctic endeavors was sealed. The expedition ship *Karluk*—already a source of grief because many believed it was not up to dealing with the Arctic ice, despite Stefansson's insistence to the contrary —was frozen in on the north coast of Alaska. Stefansson eventually disembarked with several companions to go on a ten-day hunting trip, believing, as he would claim in his book, that the *Karluk* was there to stay. But, within twenty-four hours, a storm carried the ship away, while Stefansson, already far off in the distance, watched helplessly. Forced to drift with the ice for the next six months, the *Karluk* was crushed and sank in the Chukchi Sea, leaving the twenty-five people aboard, most of them inexperienced in Arctic travel, to fend for themselves. With little prepared food and inadequate clothing (Stefansson did a poor job of outfitting the expedition), one group set off on its own and disappeared. Another four headed to Herald Island and died there. The third group, which included eleven scientists and five Inuit, made it to Wrangel Island. Newfoundlander Bob Bartlett and the Inuk Kataktovik traveled to the Siberian mainland, looking for help. When a rescue party finally arrived in September 1914, two had already died and one person had committed suicide, making the tragedy of the *Karluk* the worst in the Arctic since the disappearance of the *Erebus* and *Terror*.

*The* Karluk *caught in the ice pack off Camden Bay, Alaska, in August 1913. The crew is pumping water aboard from a fresh water pool on the ice.*

Despite all that he accomplished in the course of the next five years and all of the international publicity he directed towards Canada's interests, Stefansson's decision to carry on with the expedition, and his refusal to heed calls from the government that he return, earned him the wrath of many of his colleagues. That ignominy was to last until his death. So angry were some that they went to extraordinary lengths to attack Stefansson's honesty and integrity. Anderson, at one point, told the editor of the *Geographical Review* that Stefansson was an "international socialist," a "coward" and a "bounder," who thought himself "a cosmopolitan superman above country." He was, he added, "a Pacifist, disclaiming he owed anything to a country which brought him out of poverty, allowed him to sponge his education through state universities and three years of Harvard." On a more professional level, Anderson pushed the view that Stefansson had never intended to return to the *Karluk* once he had left it; Stefansson's plan, he charged, was to look out only for himself and his own interests.

*Mukpie, a native of Point Barrow, Alaska, was the youngest person aboard the* Karluk *and one of the survivors. Altogether eleven men died, including five in the scientific party, after the* Karluk *was crushed by ice.*

It was evident that much of Anderson's vitriol stemmed from his intense distaste for the way Stefansson promoted himself at the expense of the other expedition members. His views were given added credence by people like Jenness and Danish ethnologist Knud Rasmussen. Both were more formidable foes of Stefansson than Anderson was, insofar as they could raise serious doubts not only about whether he really did have the ability to live off the land, as Jenness would do in the journal *Science*, but also about his scientific theories and research. In fact, sixty years after the *Karluk* was crushed by ice, emotions regarding Stefansson ("Stef" to his friends, "Windjammer" to his critics) were still running high. It was then that William Laird McKinlay, one of the survivors of the *Karluk* tragedy, finally broke his self-imposed silence on the subject to clear up what he described as "inaccuracies" that Stefansson had promoted about the whole affair.

This bitter controversy had little impact on Stefansson's colorful career in the United States as a great intellect. There, he settled comfortably into a university life, and as one of his biographers described it, was "a living legend" until his death in 1962. But the Canadian Arctic expedition virtually ended any hope of Stefansson's ever personally leading another sovereignty mission to the Arctic for Canada, save for an ill-advised attempt to claim Wrangel Island in 1922, which he pursued from afar and without the Canadian government's having a clear idea of his plans. The Canadian government simply wouldn't trust Stefansson's motives after he returned south in 1918. When, for example, he proposed another expedition in 1920, advising government officials that the "Americans are at last after the lands north of Canada because they want them as territorial possessions," he was put off time and time again, until the government finally refused. An upcoming election, they suggested, was the reason. Behind closed doors, however, they discussed the possibility that Stefansson might actually betray Canada's sovereignty claims if they hired him. "Stefansson knows the weaknesses of Canada's claims as well as we do," said J.B. Harkin, the commissioner of dominion parks. "He is generally regarded as being more of an American than a Canadian."

The Stefansson affair stalled Canada's more concerted efforts to assert sovereignty over the Arctic for many years. One of Stefansson's associates described what followed as the "feud that froze the Arctic." In essence, the Arctic was left largely to the small RCMP force detachments to manage for the next several decades, too tall an order, it turned out, for what was essentially a small group of law-enforcement officers. According to Jenness, the government's Arctic policy following the Canadian Arctic expedition was "sterile" and "steering without a compass." The Inuit, he said, were merely "wards of the police," at a time when their traditional economy was falling apart and their health deteriorating as a result of disease. "The times," he said, "called for a hold-the-line policy devoid of any new experiments or adventures that might involve the government in extra expenditures. The police could continue as before to uphold Canada's sovereignty in the Arctic and maintain peace...the missions, supported by small subsidies, could provide all the hospitalization and rudimentary education that the Eskimos required; while the traders, gently regulated, could take care of their economic welfare."

To be sure, the RCMP domination of the Canadian North did not put an end to Canadian exploration in the Arctic. In the years leading up to the Second World War, the Geological Survey of Canada, which was founded in 1842, but largely limited in its activities to the central regions of the country before the turn of the century, had undertaken significant explorations in the Yukon and Northwest Territories. The RCMP itself had also done some exploring in the course of its duties during this time. One trip by Staff Sergeant A.H. Joy in 1929 was a remarkable 1700-mile (2737-km) sledge journey from Dundas Harbour at the mouth of Lancaster Sound to Melville Island, then back again by way of the Queen Elizabeth Islands and the Ellesmere Island ice-cap. Another by Constable C.L Delisle and an Inuk companion used dogs to travel 3551-miles (5717-km) from Pond Inlet on Baffin Island across Fury and Hecla Strait to Melville Peninsula, south to Repulse Bay and then back to Pond Inlet. Only the Danish ethnologist Knud Rasmussen had traveled a greater distance in the far north. Between 1921 and 1924, he and fellow scientists along with two Greenland Inuit traveled from Hudson Bay to the Bering Sea in the course of the Fifth Thule Expedition.

The most famous of the Canadian explorations in the Arctic was led by Henry Larsen, an RCMP skipper who had come from the same district of Norway as Amundsen. Between 1940 and 1942, he and his crew became the first to navigate the Northwest Passage waters from west to east. They also became the first to navigate the Passage in both directions when they brought their 104-foot (32-metre), 150-horsepower diesel-driven schooner *St. Roch* home to Vancouver via the Northwest Passage in 1944. The voyages were for Larsen the fulfillment of a lifelong passion. He had joined the RCMP in 1928, a year after attaining Canadian citizenship, to live just this kind of northern life. Quiet, modest, but exceedingly capable both as a navigator and outdoorsman, he credited Stefansson's books for many of his cold weather skills. Although Larsen was anything but a political man, he believed that it was "only natural" that responsibility for demonstrating Canada's sovereignty over the Arctic waters would be entrusted to the RCMP, given the fact that it had established its first detachment in the Arctic in 1903. "When the government had sent an expedition into the Arctic for the purpose of patrolling, exploring, and establishing authority on the northwest coast of Hudson Bay and the islands to the north," he said, "it was understood that these islands were being looked after by Canada. They had been discovered by British explorers in the early 1800s, but our trip would be the first time in twenty-three years that a Canadian ship had visited many parts of the Arctic Archipelago."

*Photograph of a Coronation Gulf Eskimo was taken on the Canadian Arctic expedition, May 26, 1913.*

*Muskoxen, which occur naturally only in the Canadian Arctic and Greenland, stand in a defensive position. They were used as a food source by some of the early explorers.*

Still, for all that Larsen and others had accomplished, the Canadian government had, as Jenness and others have suggested, little to be proud of in its management of the Arctic in the first sixty years of the twentieth century. One in six Inuit was hospitalized in the 1950s as a result of tuberculosis. Sporadic outbreaks of polio and influenza had wiped out families. In addition, game populations had been so badly decimated by both the whalers and the Hudson's Bay Company trade that the trapping of beaver and the hunting of muskoxen and whales had to be banned for certain periods in some areas. By 1939, not one native person was employed in the highly lucrative mining industry. While the Canadian government did in 1931 ban commercial harvesting of bowhead whales, the action had come too late to allow for a meaningful repopulation of the animals. On the other hand, the so-called philanthropic decision to move the Inoucdjouac Inuit from northern Quebec to the High Arctic was in reality a political decision designed primarily to strengthen the sovereignty interests of the country.

"No, there are no more sunny continents—no more islands of the blest—hidden under the far horizon, tempting the dreamer over the undiscovered sea; nothing but those weird and tragic shores, those cliffs of everlasting ice and mainlands of frozen snow, which have never produced anything to us but late and sad discovery of the depths of human heroism, patience, and bravery, such as imagination could scarcely dream of."

—Blackwood's *Edinburgh Magazine*, November 1855

# EPILOGUE

To count up the ships, the overland treks and the victims is one way of summarizing the enduring mystique of the Northwest Passage. There were, of course, hundreds of them—too many perhaps to glorify what geographical knowledge and meager material gain was attained over a period of five centuries. And the failure of most of the chroniclers of these voyages to recognize the contributions of North American aboriginals like Matonabbee, Akaitcho, Augustus and Ouligbuck raises some serious questions about discoveries of a land or a route that had been familiar to a people for centuries. On the other hand, anyone who has stood on that low height of land on Banks Island which McClure used as a perch to look for a rescue party in 1852 and 1853, or hiked the gravel shoreline of Fury Beach on Somerset Island where one of Parry's ships was crushed by ice, or traveled for that matter a short distance in the path of Hearne or Franklin across the open tundra, can't help but admire the human spirit, the perseverance, and the nerve that drove these men on.

The Northwest Passage was, in reality, not so much a short-cut to the Orient as it was a stage for Western man to play out roles he could not play at home. For the ordinary seaman, joining the search was a reprieve from a tedious existence in which anonymity and poverty were assured. For the leaders of the expeditions, it offered fame in societies where social status was largely determined by birth. And for nations like England, Norway, Canada, the United States and others, it was the backdrop against which the skills and aspirations of its people could be tested and proven.

*The shoreline of Grise Fiord, Canada's most northerly Inuit community.*

But as much as the Northwest Passage was a stage on which courage, ideas and the desires of men and nations could be played out, most of the actors in these efforts could not help but bring their world with them. It was their illusions, preconceptions, and dreams that made the idea of an Arctic route to the Orient so alluring for so long. In the scene that set the stage for the search for the Northwest Passage, the Vikings were mesmerized by mirages on their northwest horizon and set out in spite of fears that maelstroms and whirlpools would swallow their boats. Later on, Cabot, Martin Frobisher, and Henry Hudson chose to put their faith in speculative cartography to imagine lands that did not exist. And then there was Alexander Mackenzie who was convinced that the river that was eventually named after him flowed into the Pacific Ocean. Illusions, of course, produced victims like the 129 men on the last Franklin expedition, but they also led to a process of elimination in which the geographic reality of the New World was unfolded and the course of the Northwest Passage eventually found.

Twentieth century explorers like Roald Amundsen and Vilhjalmur Stefansson owed a great deal to these early dreamers, for instead of having to speculate about the great unknown, they were left to fit together the last few pieces of the puzzle. More than anyone else, Stefansson exploited this advantage. With nearly the whole geographic picture in front of him, he was able to speculate with authority on what might be and what was possible in the Arctic and sub-Arctic world. In the natural gas flare-off that he observed on the Athabasca River in 1906, for example, he saw "the torch of science lighting the way of civilization and economic development." In the strawberries that the missionaries grew at Fort Providence, he saw agriculture some day spreading to the North. And while watching beluga whales break through the ice in the Beaufort Sea, he envisioned a time when submarines would power their way through the Arctic waters, making countries like England, Norway, and Japan closer neighbors. In all three cases, Stefansson's predictions proved to be accurate.

As the nation that inherited the Northwest Passage prior to the turn of the century, Canada has had trouble embracing the vision of the North that Stefansson foisted upon it. With the exception of its aboriginal people, southern Canadians have generally looked northwards with a certain degree of stage fright, largely because they still cling to some of the illusions that victimized the nineteenth-century explorers. The North may be mysterious and beautiful, but Canadians also see it as cold, barren, and dangerous. Fewer than 10 000 non-native Canadians live above the tree-line, an area which represents about a quarter of the country's land mass. No wonder Stefansson at one point complained to the Canadian humorist Stephen Leacock that his book, *The Friendly Arctic*, had sold more copies in Cleveland than it had in all of Canada and the British territories.

Canadian geographer Louis-Edmond Hamelin referred to this combination of idealization and pessimism as the double-illusion. The term also aptly describes the contradictory manner in which the Canadian government attempted to assert its sovereignty over the Northwest Passage during the past century. On the one hand, for example, Canada recognized the need to control and collect tariffs from the foreign whalers fishing in the waters of the Northwest Passage; on the other, it feared that the whalers might take offence. Prior to and during the Second World War, Canada dispatched Henry Larsen

*A Coast Guard ice-breaker in the passage off Somerset Island.*

to navigate the Northwest Passage after negotiating a diplomatic settlement with Norway over the Sverdrup land claims. Yet shortly afterwards, it turned to the United States to help defend its northern borders.

The United States' contention that the Northwest Passage is an international strait has brought with it a realization in Canada that its approach to maritime issues in the Arctic has been, as Franklyn Griffiths says, "reactive, fragmented, and lacking the ability to follow through on non-urgent conditions." This approach was evident in the 1970 and 1985 Northwest Passage voyages of the American oil tanker *Manhattan* and the U.S. *Polar Sea* icebreaker. In both cases, the Americans proceeded without seeking permission or consulting with Canada. Canada, in turn, failed to follow through on a course of action that might have strengthened its own claim and objections to such transits. Canada, for example, vowed to establish a national park in the area of Lancaster Sound, build a Polar 8 icebreaker to patrol Arctic waters, and enforce the Arctic Waters Pollution Prevention Act against any foreign ship that might pollute the waters of the Northwest Passage. However, with the waning of public interest in northern issues, the national park in Lancaster Sound never materialized, plans for a Polar 8 have been put on hold indefinitely, and in the summer of 1990, the Canadian government exempted the U.S. *Polar Sea* from the Arctic Waters Pollution Prevention Act as it prepared for another transit through the Northwest Passage.

Both Canada and the United States have agreed to disagree over the legal status of the Northwest Passage. But there are signs that the stalemate may some day be resolved amicably. The United States has recently agreed to at least inform the Canadian government whenever a ship under its flag undertakes another transit. More importantly, however, the Northwest Passage could once again become the focal point of international cooperation just as it did during the search for the missing Franklin men. Soviet Union president Mikhail Gorbachev suggested in 1987, for example, that the circumpolar Arctic become a "zone of peace" in which no military activity would be allowed. It is an idea that the world's Inuit put forward in 1982. The Canadian government, on the other hand, has attempted to focus world attention on global pollution and climatic warming that has had and will continue to have dramatic consequences for the Arctic environment. To mitigate those consequences, Canada has encouraged scientists from all over the world to collaborate in an effort to find solutions.

With the growing importance of the Northwest Passage in the world economy, however, comes the danger of environmental degradation. Should the Northwest Passage some day become a year-round route for the transportation of vast amounts of oil, natural gas and minerals that lie beneath Arctic lands and waters, for example, a large oil spill could result in a catastrophe. The seriousness of a spill would be further compounded if it occurred near one of the wildlife-rich polynyas of the Northwest Passage in winter or spring when the ice is still present. The spill of the Exxon tanker *Valdez* highlighted the fact that no country has the ability to deal with an oil spill on the open sea. The world can be assured that a similar accident in the Northwest Passage, where winds and currents could carry the contaminated ice to more sensitive shorelines, would make clean-up and containment a logistical nightmare.

The legacy of the Northwest Passage is a complicated one, rife with human drama in surreal landscapes, of courage and recklessness in the face of danger, and of heartache and reward in the pursuit of material wealth. Still, Fritdjof Nansen's proclamation in 1911 that nowhere has man moved more slowly, stepped forward with so much trouble, endured so many privations and suffering with the promise of so little material gain, remains relevant today. The allure of the Passage lives on for those who continue to seek material wealth, for those who hunger for adventure, and for those who look for spiritual inspiration in a land and seascape which is as sublime and picturesque as that in any part of the world.

# CHRONOLOGY

*1497*
*1498*
**John Cabot**, authorized by Henry VII of England, makes the first recorded landfall on the North American continent since the Norse.

*1500*
*1501*
**Gaspar Corte-Real**, with two ships, reaches Newfoundland. The next year, with three ships, he explores the Labrador coast. Two of the ships return to Lisbon, but Corte-Real's ship is never seen again.

*1502*
**Miguel Corte-Real**, Gaspar's brother, sails towards Newfoundland with three ships. He and his ship fail to show up at their appointed rendezvous. Another expedition sent out the following year to find the crew returned without any clues of their whereabouts.

*1508*
**Thomas Aubert**, a French explorer, sails to the New World in *La Pensée* in 1506.

*1509*
**Sebastian Cabot**, in two ships, claims that he has made a voyage in search of the Northwest Passage. New evidence suggests that his vessels reached Labrador and entered Hudson Bay.

*1516*
**John Rastell** organizes an expedition to search for the Northwest Passage but is unable to find crews willing to carry out his plan to set up a base in Newfoundland.

*1524*
**Giovanni Da Verrazano**, aboard the French ship *La Dauphine*, journeys up the Atlantic coastline from Chesapeake Bay to Newfoundland in search of the Northwest Passage.

*1524–25*
**Esteban Gómez**, a Portuguese navigator in search of the Northwest Passage, explores the eastern seaboard from Florida to Newfoundland.

*1527–28*
**John Rut**, in *Mary of Guilford*, sails as far north as Labrador before heading south to the Caribbean.

*1534*
*1535*
**Jacques Cartier**, with two ships, explores and charts the Gulf of St. Lawrence. The following year, with three ships, he explores the St. Lawrence River.

*1553*
**Sir Hugh Willoughby** and **Richard Chancellor**, in three ships, search for the Northeast Passage.

*1555–56*
**Richard Chancellor**, in the *Edward Bonaventure*, searches for the Northeast Passage.

*1556–57*
**Stephen Borough**, in the *Searchthrift*, sights the Kara Sea while searching for the Northeast Passage.

*1576*
*1577*
*1578*
**Martin Frobisher**, with two ships, explores Frobisher Bay while searching for the Northwest Passage. He returns in 1577 and 1578 to mine what he believes to be gold, but on each journey returns to England with worthless rock.

*1580*
**Arthur Pet** and **William Jackman**, in the *George* and *William*, search for the Northeast Passage.

*1584*
**Oliver Brunel**, financed by other Dutchmen, searches for the Northeast Passage.

*1585*
*1586*
*1587*
**John Davis**, in the *Sunneshine* and *Mooneshine*, sails north along the Greenland coast, then crosses the strait that bears his name to Baffin Island near Cumberland Sound. He follows a similar route the following year, but is stopped by a massive ice floe. On his final voyage, with three ships, he again follows the Greenland coast before heading west to Baffin Island, where he noted the entrances to Frobisher Bay and Hudson Strait before heading home.

*1594*
**Cornelius Nay, Brent Tetgailes, Jan H. Van Linschoten** and **Willem Barents** search for the Northeast Passage.

*1595*
**Cornelius Nay** and **Willem Barents** lead an expedition of six ships and a yacht to discover the Northeast Passage.

*1596–97*
**Willem Barents, Jacob Van Heemskerck** and **Jan C. Rup**, searching for the Northeast Passage, discover Spitsbergen and Novaya Zemlya. First European expedition to survive an Arctic winter.

*1602*
**George Weymouth**, in the *Discovery*, reaches Hudson Strait.

*1605*
**John Cunningham, James Hall** and **John Knight**, in three ships, explore the west coast of Greenland for Christian IV of Denmark.

*1606*

**John Knight**, in the *Hopewell*, searches for the Northwest Passage along the coast of Labrador.

**James Hall**, with five ships, is sent by Christian IV of Denmark to Greenland to conduct mineralogical explorations.

*1607*

**Henry Hudson**, aboard the *Hopewell*, searches for the Northeast Passage for the English Muscovy Company.

**James Hall**, with two ships, is prevented by ice from reaching Greenland.

*Henry Hudson*

*1609*
*1610–11*

**Henry Hudson**, aboard the *Hopewell*, searches for a Northeast Passage for the Dutch East India Company. He sails in the *Half Moon* up the west coast of Norway before sailing west to North America, where he travels up the Hudson River in 1609. In 1610, Hudson, in the *Discovery*, is the first European to sail into the bay that bears his name. He and eight others are set adrift in the bay after a mutiny in 1611.

*1612*

**James Hall** and **William Baffin**, in the *Patience* and *Heart's Ease*, explore the west coast of Greenland in search of the Northwest Passage.

*1612–13*

**Thomas Button**, with two ships, searches for Henry Hudson and the Passage. He crosses Hudson Bay and winters at the mouth of the Nelson River.

*1613*

**Benjamin Joseph** and **William Baffin**, with seven ships, search for the Northeast Passage.

*1614*

**Benjamin Joseph** and **William Baffin**, with a fleet of thirteen ships, search for the Northeast Passage.

**William Gibbons**, in the *Discovery*, intends to search for the Northwest Passage through Hudson Bay but is blocked by ice.

*1615*

**Robert Bylot** and **William Baffin**, aboard the *Discovery*, explore the entrance to Hudson Strait.

*1616*

**Robert Bylot** and **William Baffin**, aboard the *Discovery*, explore Smith Sound, Jones Sound and Lancaster Sound.

*1619–20*

**Jens Munk**, a Dane, over-winters at the mouth of the Churchill River.

*1625*

**William Hawkridge**, with two ships, enters Hudson Strait to search for the Northwest Passage.

*1631*

**Luke Foxe**, aboard the *Charles*, explores Hudson Bay.

*1631–32*

**Thomas James**, aboard the *Henrietta Maria*, over-winters in James Bay.

*1719 (?) – 22*

**James Knight**, with the *Albany* and *Discovery*, attempts to take refuge on Marble Island in Hudson Bay when the ships are damaged. After two winters, there are no survivors. Presumably, they all starved.

*1728*

**Vitus Bering**, a Danish navigator employed by Russia, discovers the strait named after him.

*1737*

**James Napper** and **Robert Crow**, in the *Churchill*, search for the Northwest Passage.

*1741–42*

**Christopher Middleton**, with two ships, searches for the Northwest Passage in Hudson Bay.

*1746–47*

**William Moor** and **Francis Smith** explore Hudson Bay.

*1753*
*1754*

**Charles Swaine**, in the *Argo*, makes two voyages in search of the Northwest Passage.

*1769*
*1770*
*1770–72*

**Samuel Hearne** makes three overland journeys to find the Northwest Passage. On the last one with his Indian guide Matonabbee, he reaches the mouth of the Coppermine River and becomes the first European to see the Arctic Ocean north of the continental mainland.

*1773*

**Constantine Phipps** searches for the Northwest Passage by heading north from Spitsbergen towards the Pole.

*1776*

**Richard Pickerskill**, in the *Lion*, begins a mission to protect British whalers in the Davis Strait, as well as to find the Northwest Passage.

*1777*

**Walter Young**, in the *Lion*, searches for the Northwest Passage.

*1789*

**Alexander Mackenzie** is guided down the Mackenzie River to the Beaufort Sea by native guides.

*1817*
**William Scoresby**, a whaler, explores the Arctic waters around Greenland.

*1818*
**John Ross**, with the *Isabella* and *Alexander*, is turned back by the mythical Croker Mountains, which he believes block passage through Lancaster Sound.

**David Buchan**, with John Franklin as second-in-command, in the *Dorothea* and *Trent*, are forced back by storms in an attempt to sail north from Spitsbergen to the Pole.

*Sir William Edward Parry*

*1819–20*
**William Edward Parry**, with the *Hecla* and *Griper*, reaches Melville Sound. The crew earned the £5000 parliamentary bounty for reaching 110 degrees west.

*1819–22*
**John Franklin** leads a disastrous overland expedition and reaches Point Turnagain. Eleven members die en route and the remainder are saved by the intervention of Indian guide Akaitcho.

*1821–23*
*1824–25*
**William Edward Parry**, with two ships, reaches Fury and Hecla Strait. In 1824 he tries again to find the Passage, but the *Fury* is wrecked on the east coast of Somerset Island and he is forced to return to England in the *Hecla*.

*1824–25*
**George Lyon**, aboard the *Griper*, tries to reach Point Turnagain, but is unsuccessful.

*1825–27*
**John Franklin** leads a second overland expedition. He takes a group west and maps nearly 1000 miles (1600 km) of coastline to Icy Cape. John Richardson leads a second group east and reaches the mouth of the Coppermine River.

*1825–28*
**Frederick W. Beechey** takes the *Blossom* to Icy Cape in an unsuccessful attempt to rendezvous with Franklin's overland expedition.

*1829–33*
**John Ross**, in the *Victory*, makes a second expedition in search of the Passage. Ross and his crew are forced to spend four winters at Victory Harbour and Fury Beach.

*1833–35*
*1836–37*
**George Back** leads an overland expedition from Great Slave Lake down the Great Fish River to the Arctic coast. Three years later, in the *Terror*, he enters Hudson Bay where his ship is nearly crushed by the ice.

*1837–39*
**Peter Dease** and **Thomas Simpson** survey the Arctic coast for the Hudson's Bay Company.

*1845*
**John Franklin**, commanding the *Erebus* and *Terror*, searches for the Northwest Passage.

*1846–47*
**Hudson Bay Company** sponsors an overland search to verify and continue the earlier survey conducted by Dease and Simpson.

*1848–49*
**James Clark Ross**, in the *Enterprise* and *Investigator*, searches for Franklin.

*1848–49*
**Thomas Moore**, in the *Plover*, searches for Franklin.

**Robert Sheldon**, in the *Nancy Dawson*, searches for Franklin.

*1848–50*
**Henry Kellett**, in the *Herald*, searches for Franklin.

*1848–51*
**W.J.S. Pullen** searches for Franklin along the Arctic coastline as far as the Mackenzie delta.

**John Rae** and **John Richardson** canoe the Mackenzie River to the Arctic coast and explore Victoria Island in search of Franklin.

*1849–50*
**James Saunders**, in the *North Star*, searches for Franklin.

*1849*
**Robert Goodsir**, in the *Advice*, searches for Franklin.

*1850*
**Charles Codrington Forsythe**, in the *Prince Albert*, searches for Franklin.

*1850–51*
**Edwin J. De Haven**, with the *Advance* and *Rescue*, travels with Elisha Kent Kane as surgeon on the U.S. Grinnell expedition in search of Franklin.

**Horatio Austin** commands a four-ship expedition in search of Franklin.

**William Penny** in the *Lady Franklin* and **Alexander Stewart** in the *Sophia* search for Franklin.

**Sir John Ross**, in the *Felix*, leads a private expedition in search of Franklin.

*1850–54*
**Robert McClure**, in the *Investigator*, searches for Franklin via the Bering Strait and discovers the final link in the Northwest Passage.

*1850–55*
**Richard Collinson**, in the *Enterprise*, searches the western Arctic for Franklin.

*1851–52*
**William Kennedy** and **Joseph Rene Bellot**, in the *Prince Albert*, head a search expedition financed by Lady Franklin.

*1852*
**Charles Frederick**, in the *Amphitrite*, searches for Franklin.

**Edward Inglefield**, in the *Isabel*, explores Smith and Jones sounds while searching for Franklin.

*1852–55*
**Rochfort Maguire**, in the *Plover*, searches for Franklin.

*1852–54*
**Sir Edward Belcher**, in the *Assistance*, leads a five-ship expedition to find Franklin, sponsored by the British Admiralty.

**Henry Kellet**, in the *Resolute*, under Belcher's command, rescues McClure and the survivors aboard the *Investigator*.

*1853*
**William Fawkner**, in the *Breadalbane*; the ship sinks off Beechey Island.

**J. Elliot**, in the *Diligence*, searches for Franklin.

*1853–54*
**John Rae**, in the *North Pole* and *Magnet*, conducts a survey of the Arctic coast for the Hudson's Bay Company and receives reward for bringing back evidence of the fate of the Franklin expedition.

*1853–55*
**Elisha Kent Kane**, in the *Advance*, leads an American expedition in search of Franklin.

*1857–59*
**Leopold McClintock**, in the *Fox*, confirms earlier Inuit reports as told to John Rae that the Franklin crew had perished on King William Island. He brings home

*Roald Amundsen*

the only written documentation relating to the voyage of the *Erebus* and *Terror*.

*1860–61*
**Isaac Hayes** searches for an open polar sea.

*1860–63*
*1864–69*
*1871–73*
**Charles Francis Hall** sets out in search of Franklin with a whaling fleet, but makes it only as far as Frobisher Bay. On his third journey, in the *Polaris*, he undertakes to reach the Pole, but is poisoned and dies.

*1875*
**Allen Young**, in the *Pandora*, conducts a private expedition to navigate the Passage in a single season. He is unsuccessful.

*1878–80*
**Frederick Schwatka** conducts an overland trek in search of further clues to the fate of John Franklin. Accompanied by

twelve Inuit, he travels 3252 miles (5232 km) by sled.

*1903–06*
**Roald Amundsen**, in the *Gjoa*, makes the first full transit of the Northwest Passage from east to west.

*1923–24*
**Knud Rasmussen**, with two Inuit companions, follows the Northwest Passage by land on a scientific expedition from Hudson Bay to Bering Strait.

*1940–42*
*1944*
**Henry Larsen**, in the *St. Roch*, an RCMP schooner, makes the first west-to-east passage. In 1944, he returns west and becomes the first to make the journey in one season as well as the first to navigate the Passage in both directions.

*1954*
**O.C.S. Robertson**, in the CCGS Labrador, an icebreaker, makes the voyage as part of the first circumnavigation of North America.

*1956*
**T.C. Pullen** in CCGS *Labrador* navigates the Passage from east to west.

*1957*
**H.L. Woods** and others in the USCG *Storis*, *Bramble* and *Spar* make the first passage by squadron.

*1960*
**G.P. Steel III**, in the USS *Seadragon*, commands the first submarine to make an east-to-west transit of the Northwest Passage.

*1962*
**J.F. Calvert**, in the USS *Skate*, makes an east-to-west passage via submarine.

*1967*
**P.M. Fournier**, in the CCGS *John A. Macdonald*, makes an east-to-west passage as part of a circumnavigation of North America.

*1969*
**P.M. Fournier**, in the CCGS *John A. Macdonald*, escorts the *Manhattan*.

**R.A. Steward**, in the *Manhattan*, the largest ship to navigate the Northwest Passage, leads a special experiment to see if the transport of bulk oil from Alaska would be feasible through the Passage.

*1970*
**P. Brick** and **D.W. Butler**, in the CSS *Baffin* and the CSS *Hudson*, make a west-to-east transit.

*1975*
**P. Kalis**, in the CCGS *Skidegate*, makes a west-to-east transit.

**G. Yarn**, in the CCGS *John A. Macdonald*, makes a west-to-east transit.

**R. Dickinson** and **K. Maro**, in the *Pandora II* and the *Theta*, make a west-to-east transit.

*1976*
**P. Pelian** and **F. Chouinard**, in the CCGS *J.E. Bernier*, make a west-to-east transit.

*1976–78*
**R. Bouvier**, in the *J.E. Bernier II*, a ketch, makes an east-to-west transit.

*1977*
**W. De Roos**, in the *Williwaw* (Netherlands), a 42-foot (13-m) ketch, makes the first single-handed passage from east to west.

*1978*
**P.M.R. Toomey**, in the CCGS *Pierre Radisson*, makes a west-to-east transit.

*1979*
**G. Burdock**, in the CCGS *Louis St. Laurent*, makes an east-to-west passage to assist CCGS *Franklin*, which was trapped by ice in Viscount Melville Sound.

*1980*
**E. Chasse**, in the CCGS *J.E. Bernier*, makes a transit while circumnavigating North America.

**R. Jones**, aboard *Pandora II*, a hydrographic research vessel, makes a transit from west to east.

*1981*
**F. Mauger** makes a west-to-east transit aboard CSS *Hudson*.

*1981–83*
**K. Horie**, aboard the Japanese sloop *Mermaid*, makes an east-to-west transit.

*1983*
**J. Dool**, aboard *Arctic Shiko*, makes a west-to-east transit.

*1983–88*
**W. Jacobson**, aboard the French vessel, *The Vagabond II*, makes a west-to-east transit.

**J. Bockstoce**, aboard the U.S. motor yacht *Belvedere*, makes a west-to-east transit.

*1984*
**J.A. Strand**, aboard *Polar Ice*, makes a west-to-east transit.

**H. Nilsson**, and **T.C. Pullen** in the *Lindblad Explorer*, the first commercial passenger vessel to make a transit from east-to-west.

*1985*
**Heinz Aye**, aboard the commercial passenger ship *World Discoverer*, makes a west-to-east transit.

**J.T. Howell**, aboard USCG *Polar Sea*, makes an east-to-west transit.

*1986–88*
**Jeff MacInnis** and **Mike Beedell**, aboard *Perception*, a Hobie catamaran sailboat, make a partial transit of the Northwest Passage.

*1988*
**S. Gomes**, aboard CCGS *Henry Larsen*, on its maiden voyage, makes a west-to-east transit.

**R. Mellis**, aboard CCGS *Martha L. Black*, makes a west-to-east transit.

**Heinz Aye**, aboard MV *Society Explorer*, a Bahamas-registered passenger ship, makes a west-to-east transit.

**P.R. Taylor**, aboard USCG *Polar Star*, makes a transit.

**Ron Colby**, aboard *Canmar Explorer II*, makes a transit.

*1989*
**R. Hammond**, aboard USCG *Polar Star*, makes a transit.

# SOURCE NOTES

The following titles were used in the development of the manuscript. Full titles are given in the first citation; subsequent citations are by short-form reference. Unpublished titles and references are also cited.

*General Reference*
Cooke, Alan and Holland, Clive. *The Exploration of Northern Canada*, Toronto, The Arctic History Press, 1978.

*Pilot of Arctic Canada*. Ottawa, Department of Energy, Mines and Resources, 1970.

*Introduction*
Government of Canada, Canadian Coast Guard Service. "Full and Partial Transits of the Northwest Passage," personal correspondence, 1989.

Loomis, Chauncey C. "The Arctic Sublime," in U.C. Knoepflmacher and Tennyson, G.B., *Nature and the Victorian Imagination*, University of California Press, 1977.

Mackinnon, C.S. "The Wintering Over of Royal Navy Ships in the Canadian Arctic, 1819–1876," in *Beaver* Vol. 315, No. 3. 1984/85.

Nansen, Fridtjof. *In Northern Mists*, Volume One, Arthur Chater, trans., New York, Frederick A. Stokes, 1911.

*Polar Press*. "Cruise Ship Navigates Northwest Passage," Associated Press report, December 1984.

*Chapter One*
Amundsen, Roald. *The Northwest Passage: Being the Record of A Voyage of Exploration on the Ship* Gjoa *1903–1907*, (two volumes), London, Archibald Constable, 1908.

Back, George. *Narrative of the Arctic Land Expedition to the Mouth of the Great Fish River*, Edmonton, Hurtig, 1970 (reprint, originally published 1836).

Gagné, Raymond C. "Spatial Concepts in the Eskimo Language," in *Eskimo of the Canadian Arctic*, Victor Valentine and Frank Vallee, eds., The Carleton Library, No. 41. Toronto, McClelland and Stewart, 1968.

Gombrich, E.H. *The Story of Art*. London, Phaidon Press, twelfth edition, 1972.

Grant, Shelagh D. *Sovereignty or Security?* Vancouver, University of British Columbia Press, 1988.

Griffiths, Franklyn. *Politics of the Northwest Passage*, Montreal and Kingston, McGill-Queen's University Press, 1987.

Hamelin, Louis-Edmond. *Canadian Nordicity: It's Your North, Too*, William Barr, trans., Montreal, Harvest House, 1979.

Havis, Magda and Hutchison, Thomas C. "The Smoking Hills: Natural Acidification of an Aquatic Ecosystem," in *Nature*, Vol 301, No. 5895, pp. 23–27.

Hofstadter, Richard. *The Age of Reform*, New York, Random House, 1955.

Hood, Robert. *To the Arctic by Canoe, the Journal and Paintings of Robert Hood, Midshipman With Franklin*, C. Stuart Houston, ed., Montreal and London, McGill-Queen's University Press, 1974.

Loomis, Chauncey. *The Arctic Sublime*.

Lopez, Barry. *Arctic Dreams, Imagination and Desire in a Northern Landscape*, New York, Charles Scribner's Sons, 1986.

MacLaren, I.S. "The Aesthetic Map of the North, 1845–1859," in *Arctic*, Volume 38, No. 2, pp. 89–103.

——. "where nothing moves and nothing changes, the Second Arctic Expedition of John Ross (1829–1833)," in *Dalhousie Review*, 62.

McClure, Robert. *The Discovery of the Northwest Passage*, Sherard Osborn, ed., Edmonton, Hurtig, 1969 reprint, originally published in 1856.

Markham, Clements. *Lands of Silence*, Cambridge, Cambridge University Press, 1921.

——. *The Life of Sir Leopold McClintock*. London, John Murray, 1909.

Nutt, David C. "The North Water of Baffin Bay," in *Polar Notes*, No. IX (May 1969), pp. 1–25.

Oleson, Tryggvi J. *Early Voyages and Northern Approaches, 1000–1632*, Toronto, McClelland and Stewart, 1963.

Saladin d'Anglure, Bernard. "The Route to China, Northern Europe's Arctic Delusions," in *Arctic*, Vol. 37, No. 4 pp. 446–452.

Savours, Ann. "A Very Interesting Point in Geography: The 1773 Phipps Expedition Towards the North Pole," in *Arctic*, Vol. 37, No. 4, pp. 402–427.

Sawatzky, H.L. and Lehn, W.H. "The Arctic Mirage and the Early North Atlantic," in *Science*, Vol. 192, June 25, 1976, pp. 1300–1305.

Stefansson, Vilhjalmur. *The Friendly Arctic: The Story of Five Years in Polar Regions*, New York, MacMillan, 1921.

——. *The Northward Course of Empire*, New York, Harcourt, Brace and Co. 1922.

Stirling, Ian and Cleator, Holly, eds. *Polynyas in the Canadian Arctic*, Occasional Paper No. 45, Canadian Wildlife Service, 1981.

Wiebe, Rudy. *Playing Dead: A Contemplation Concerning the Arctic*, Edmonton, NeWest, 1989.

Wonders, William. "Unrolling the Map of Canada's Arctic," in *A Century of Canada's Arctic Islands 1880–1980*, Morris Zaslow, ed., Ottawa, The Royal Society of Canada, 1981, pp. 1–14.

*Chapter Two*
Asher, G.M. *Henry Hudson, the Navigator* (Hakluyt Society), New York, Burt Franklin, 1860.

Davis, John. *The Voyages and Works of John Davis, the Navigator*, Albert Hastings Markham, ed., (Hakluyt Society), New York, Burt Franklin, 1889.

De Veer, Gerrit. *The Three Voyages of Willem Barents to the Arctic Regions*, (Hakluyt Society), K. Beynen, ed., New York, Burt Franklin, 1853.

Dodge, Ernest S. *Northwest by Sea*, New York, Oxford University Press, 1961.

Dunbar, Moira and Dunbar, M.J. *The History of the North Water*, Ottawa, Defence Research Establishment, University of Montreal, 1972.

Gilbert, Sir Humphrey. *A Discourse for the Discoverie for a New Passage to Cathia*, London, 1576.

Hakluyt, Richard. *The Principal Navigations, Voiages & Discoveries of the English Nation*, facsimile reprint of 1589 original, Cambridge, (Hakluyt Society).

Hansen, Thorkild, *The Way to Hudson Bay: The Life and Times of Jens Munk*, James McFarlane and John Lynch, trans., New York, Harcourt, Brace and World Inc., 1970.

James, Thomas. *Strange and Dangerous Voyage of Captaine Thomas James*, London, Legatt, 1633.

Oleson, Tryggvi J. *Early Voyages and Northern Approaches, 1000–1632*.

Pullen, Thomas C. "The Challenge of Year-Round Navigation in the Canadian North," in *Polar Record*, Vol. 21, June 1982. pp. 73–74.

Rey, Louis. "The Evangelization of the Arctic in the Sixteenth and Early Seventeenth Centuries," in *Arctic*, Vol. 37, No. 4.

Scoresby, William. *An Account of the Arctic Regions, with a History and Description of the Northern Whale Fishery*, Augustus Kelley, New York, 1969 reprint of 1820 original.

Wallis, Helen. "England's Search for the Northern Passages in the Sixteenth and Early Seventeenth Centuries," in *Arctic*, Vol. 37, No. 4.

*Chapter Three*
Back, George. *Narrative of the Arctic Land Expedition to the Mouth of the Great Fish River*.

Berton, Pierre. *The Arctic Grail: The Quest for the North West Passage and the North Pole 1818–1909*, Toronto, McClelland and Stewart, 1988.

Bliss, Michael. "Conducted Tour," in *The Beaver*, April/May 1989.

Dobbs, Arthur. *An Account of the Countries Adjoining to Hudson's Bay, In the North-West Part of America… With an Abstract of Captain Middleton's Journal and Observations Upon His Behaviour During His Voyage Since His Return…*. London, S.R. Publishers, 1967 reprint of 1744 original.

Dodge, Ernest S. *The Polar Rosses*, London, Faber and Faber, 1973.

Franklin, John. *Narrative of a Journey to the Shores of the Polar Sea, in the Years 1819, 1820, 1821, 1822*, New York, Greenwood Press, facsimile of 1823 edition.

——. *Narrative of a Second Expedition to the Shores of the Polar Sea in the Years 1825, 1826, 1827,* Edmonton, Hurtig, 1971 reprint of 1828 original.

Hearne, Samuel. *A Journey from Prince of Wales Fort in Hudson's Bay to the Northern Ocean...* Richard Glover, ed., Toronto, Macmillan, 1958 reprint of 1795 edition.

King, Richard. *Narrative of a Journey to the Shores of the Arctic Ocean, in 1833, 1834, and 1835, under the Command of Captain George Back, R.N.,* London, Richard Bentley, 1836.

——. *The Franklin Expedition from First to Last,* London, John Churchill, 1855.

Lopez, Barry. *Arctic Dreams.*

Mackenzie, Alexander. *Exploring the Northwest Territory: Sir Alexander Mackenzie's Journal of a Voyage by Bark Canoe from Lake Athabasca to the Pacific Ocean in the Summer of 1789,* T.H. McDonald, ed., University of Oklahoma Press, 1966.

McIlraith, John. *Life of Sir John Richardson,* London, Longmans Green, 1868.

Pyne, Stephen J. *The Ice: A Journey to Antarctic,* New York, Ballantyne Books, 1986.

*Report from the Select Committee on the Expedition to the Arctic Seas Commanded by Captain James Ross, R.N.,* London, House of Commons, 1834.

Rich, E.E. "The Road to Cathay and the Hudson's Bay Company," in *Polar Record,* Vol. 15, No. 97, 1971.

Richardson, John. *Arctic Ordeal: The Journal of John Richardson, Surgeon-Naturalist With Franklin 1820–1822,* C. Stuart Houston, ed., Montreal, McGill-Queen's University Press, 1985.

Ross, John. *Narrative of a Second Voyage in Search of a Northwest Passage and a Residence in the Arctic Regions During the Years 1829, 1830, 1831, 1832, 1833,* London, A.W. Webster, 1835.

Ross, W. Gillies and Barr, W. "Voyages in Northwest Hudson Bay 1720–1722 and the Discovery of the Knight Relics on Marble Island," in *Musk-Ox,* No. 11, 1972.

Smith, Ralph and Barr, William. "Marble Island: A Search for the Knight Expedition, August 6–15," ub *Musk-Ox,* No. 11, 1972.

Wallace, Hugh N. *The Navy, the Company, and Richard King: British Exploration in the Arctic, 1829–1860,* Montreal, McGill-Queen's, 1980.

Weekes, Mary. "Akaitcho: A Link With Franklin," in *Beaver,* Vol. 270, No. 1, 1939.

*Chapter Four*
Armstrong, Alexander. *A Personal Narrative of the Discovery of the North-West Passage; With Numerous Incidents of Travel and Adventure During Nearly Five Years' Continuous Service in the Arctic Regions While In Search of the Expedition under Sir John Franklin,* London, Hurst and Blackett, 1857.

Barrow, John. *A Chronological History of Voyages into the Arctic Regions; Undertaken Chiefly for the Purpose of Discovering a North-East, North-West, Or Polar Passages Between the Atlantic and Pacific...,* John Murray, 1818, David and Charles Reprint, 1971.

Belcher, Sir Edward. *The Last of the Arctic Voyages, Being a Narrative of the Expedition H.M.S. Assistance, Under the Command of Sir Edward Belcher, C.B. In Search of Sir John Franklin,* (two volumes), London, Lovell Reeve, 1855.

Boorstin, Daniel J. *The Discoverers,* New York, Random House, 1983.

Collinson. T.B., ed. *Journal of H.M.S. Enterprise on the Expedition in Search of Sir John Franklin's Ships by the Bering Sea, 1850–55,* London, Sampson, Low, Marston, Searle, and Rivington, London, 1889.

*Edinburgh Magazine* (Blackwood's).

Hakluyt, Richard. *Voyages and Discoveries,* Jack Beeching, ed., Penguin abridged edition, 1987.

Holland, Clive. "William Penny, 1809–92, Arctic Whaling Master," in *Polar Record,* Vol. 15, No. 94.

House of Commons. *Sessional Papers,* Reports from Committees, Vol. 7, Session 12, Dec. 1854 to Aug. 1855.

Jones, A.G.E. "Rear Admiral Sir William Edward Parry: A Different View," in *Musk-Ox,* No. 21, 1978.

MacLaren, I.S. "The Aesthetic Map of the North."

McClure, Robert. *The Discovery of the Northwest Passage.*

Miertsching, Johann. *Frozen Ships: The Arctic Diary of Johann Miertsching, 1850–1854,* L.H. Neatby, trans., Toronto, Macmillan, 1967.

Neatby, L.H. *The Search for Franklin,* London, Arthur Baker, 1970.

Parry, Ann. *Parry of the Arctic: The Life Story of Admiral Sir Edward Parry, 1790–1855,* London, Chatto and Windus, 1963.

Parry, William Edward. *Journal of a Voyage for the Discovery of a North-West Passage from the Atlantic to the Pacific Performed in the Years 1819–20 in His Majesty's Ships, Hecla and Griper,* London, John Murray, 1821.

——. *Journal of a Second Voyage for the Discovery of a North-West Passage from the Atlantic to the Pacific...,* London, John Murray, 1824.

Snow, William Parker. *Voyage of the Prince Albert in Search of Sir John Franklin: A Narrative of Everyday Life in the Arctic Seas,* London, Longman, 1851.

Stamp, Tom and Stamp, Cordelia. *William Scoresby, Arctic Scientist,* Caedmon of Whitby Press, 1975.

Stone, Ian R. "Charles Codrington Forsythe," in *Arctic,* Vol. 38, No. 4.

*The Times,* 1847–1855.

*Chapter Five*
Anderson, James. "Chief Factor James Anderson's Back River Journal of 1855," in *Canadian Field Naturalist,* Vol. 54 and 55.

Beattie, Owen and Geiger, John. *Frozen in Time: Unlocking the Secrets of the Franklin Expedition,* Saskatoon, Western Producer Prairie Books, 1987.

Belcher, Sir Edward. *The Last of the Arctic Voyages.*

Bellot, Joseph-Rene. *Memoirs of Lieutenant Joseph-Rene Bellot, With His Journal of a Voyage in the Polar Sea in Search of Sir John Franklin,* London, Hurst and Blackett, 1855.

Dodge, Ernest S. *The Polar Rosses.*

Gilder, William. *Schwatka's Search,* New York, Charles Scribner's Sons, 1881.

Hall, Charles Francis. *Life with the Eskimo: A Narrative of Arctic Experience in Search of Survivors of Sir John Franklin's Expedition,* Edmonton, Hurtig reprint, 1970.

Inglefield, E.A. *A Summer Search for Sir John Franklin With a Peep into the Polar Basin...,* London, Thomas Harrison, 1853.

Kane, Elisha Kent. *Arctic Explorations: The Second Grinnel Expedition in Search of Sir John Franklin* (two volumes), Philadelphia, Childs and Peterson, 1856.

Kennedy, William. *A Short Narrative of the Second Voyage of the Prince Albert in Search of Sir John Franklin,* London, Daloton, 1853.

Klutschak, Heinrich. *Overland to Starvation Cove, With the Inuit in Search of Franklin, 1878–1880,* William Barr, ed. and trans., Toronto, University of Toronto Press, 1987.

Loomis, Chauncey. *Weird and Tragic Shores: The Story of Charles Francis Hall,* London, Macmillan, 1972.

McClintock, Leopold. *The Voyage of the Fox in Arctic Seas,* London, John Murray, 1908.

Rae, John. *Narrative of an Expedition to the Shores of the Arctic Sea in 1846 and 1847,* Canadiana House, 1979 reprint.

Rich, E.E. *John Rae's Correspondence with the Hudson's Bay Company on Arctic Exploration, 1844–1855,* London, The Hudson's Bay Record Society, 1953.

Savelle, James and Holland, Clive. "John Ross and Bellot Strait: Personality Versus Discovery," in *Polar Record,* Vol. 23, No. 145.

Simpson, George. *Journal of Occurrences in the Athabasca Department,* Toronto, Champlain Society, 1938.

Young, William Allen. *The Two Voyages of the Pandora in 1875 and 1876,* London, Edward Stanford, 1879.

*Chapter Six*
Amagoalik, John. *Special Joint Committee on Canada's International Relations* (presentation), No. 60, April 23, 1986.

Amundsen, Roald. *My Life as an Explorer,* New York, Doubleday, 1928.

——. *The North West Passage: Being a Record of a Voyage of Exploration of the Ship Gjoa, 1903–1907.*

Audlaluk, Larry. *Inuit Relocation to Grise Fiord and Canadian Sovereignty in the High Arctic,* unpublished presentation to the Fate of the Earth Conference, Ottawa, June, 1986.

Bassett, John. *Henry Larsen,* Don Mills, Fitzhenry and Whiteside, 1980.

Berger, Carl. *Sense of Power: Studies in the Ideas of Canadian Imperialism 1867–1914,* Toronto, University of Toronto Press, 1970.

Bernier, Joseph-Elzear. *Report on the Dominion Government Expedition to the Arctic Islands and the Hudson Strait on Board the C.G.S. Arctic, 1906–1907,* Ottawa, King's Printer, 1909.

——. *Report on the Dominion Government Expedition,* Ottawa, Government Printing Bureau, 1910.

Brown, Robert Craig and Cook, Ramsay. *Canada, A Nation Transformed,* Toronto, University of Toronto Press, 1970.

Diubaldo, Richard. *Stefansson and the Canadian Arctic,* McGill-Queen's University Press, 1978.

*Edmonton Journal* 1945–1988.

*Globe and Mail* 1901–1914 and 1970–1989.

Hunt, William R. *Stef: A Biography of Vilhjalmur Stefansson,* Vancouver, University of British Columbia Press, 1986.

Jenness, Diamond. *Eskimo Administration: 11. Canada,* Arctic Institute of North America, Technical Paper, 1964.

King, W.F. *Report on the Title of Canada to Lands North of the Mainland of Canada,* Ottawa, 1909.

Low, A.P. *Cruise of the Neptune 1903–04,* Ottawa, Government Printing Bureau, 1906.

Lyall, Ernie. *Arctic Man*, Edmonton, Hurtig, 1979.

McKinlay, William Laird. Karluk: *The Great Untold Story of Arctic Exploration*, New York, St. Martin's Press, 1976.

Pullen, Thomas C. "Arctic Marine Transportation: A View From the Bridge," in *Northern Perspectives*, Vol. 11, No. 5, Dec. 1983.

Rasmussen, Knud. *Across Arctic America: Narrative of the Fifth Thule Expedition*, New York, C.P. Putnam's Sons, 1927.

Steele, Harwoode. *Policing the Arctic: The Story of the Conquest of the Arctic by the Royal Canadian Mounted Police*, Toronto, Ryerson Press, 1936.

Stefansson, V. *Friendly Arctic*.
——. *Northward Course of Empire*.
——. *The Adventure of Wrangel Island*, New York, Macmillan, 1925.

Zaslow, Morris. *The Opening of the Canadian North, 1870–1914*, Toronto, McClelland and Stewart, 1971.

*Epilogue*
Diubaldo, Richard. *Stefansson and the Canadian Arctic*.

Griffiths, Franklyn. *Politics of the Northwest Passage*.

Hamelin, Louis-Edmond. *Canadian Nordicity*.

Lopez, Barry. *Arctic Dreams*.

Nansen, Fridtjof. *In Northern Mists*.

Stefansson, Vilhjalmur. *The Friendly Arctic*.
——. *Northwest to Fortune*.
——. *Northward Course of Empire*.

Struzik, Edward. "Arctic Oases: Exploring the Mysterious Ice Holes Called Polynyas," in *Equinox*, Nov./Dec. 1989.

Young, Oran. "Global Commons: The Arctic in World Affairs," in *Technology Review*, Vol. 93, No. 2.

# INDEX

Numbers in italics refer to photographs